LA SALLE IN TEXAS

LA SALLE IN TEXAS

TEXAS A&M UNIVERSITY PRESS   COLLEGE STATION

La Salle in Texas

A TEACHER'S GUIDE FOR THE AGE OF DISCOVERY AND EXPLORATION

Pam Wheat-Stranahan

Based on *From A Watery Grave: The Discovery and Excavation of La Salle's Shipwreck*, La Belle

INCLUDES DVDS

"The Shipwreck of *La Belle*"

"Dreams of Conquest"

Two Films by Alan Govenar

DISCLAIMER
Pages in this book with the heading
"STUDENT PAGES" are intended to
be reproducible as needed. Teachers are
encouraged to make as many copies of
them as necessary; no permission for
such use is required. All other content,
including the accompanying DVD, is
protected by applicable copyright law.

LIBRARY OF CONGRESS CATALOGING-IN-PUBLICATION DATA

Wheat-Stranahan, Pam.
    La Salle in Texas : a teacher's guide for the age of discovery and exploration /
Pam Wheat-Stranahan. — 1st ed.
        p. cm.
    "Based on From a watery grave: the discovery and excavation of La Salle's
shipwreck, La Belle. Includes DVDs 'The shipwreck of La Belle,' 'Dreams of conquest,'
two films by Alan Govenar."
    Includes bibliographical references.
    ISBN-13: 978-1-58544-609-4 (pbk. : alk. paper)
    ISBN-10: 1-58544-609-2 (pbk. : alk. paper)
    1. La Salle, Robert Cavelier, sieur de, 1643–1687—Study and teaching.
2. La Belle (Frigate)—Study and teaching.   3. Shipwrecks—Texas—Matagorda
Bay—Study and teaching.   4. Matagorda Bay (Tex.)—Antiquities—Study and
teaching.   5. Excavations (Archaeology)—Study and teaching.   6. Texas—
Discovery and exploration—French—Study and teaching.   7. Texas—
History—Study and teaching.   8. Ethnology—Texas—Study and teaching.
9. America—Discovery and exploration—French—Study and teaching.
10. America—Colonization—Study and teaching.
I. Bruseth, James E. From a watery grave.   II. Title.
F352.L395   2007
976.4'01—dc22   2007003205

CONTENTS

Contents

ACKNOWLEDGMENTS

I sincerely appreciate the opportunity that Jim Bruseth gave me to serve as coordinator of Educational Programs for the La Salle Project as the Texas Historical Commission (THC) began work on *La Belle* in 1996. My job was multi-faceted. I coordinated the itinerary of an exhibit prepared by the Corpus Christi Museum of Science and History, trained teachers and docents who would introduce students to the exhibit, created a web site for teacher resources and lessons for educators, and performed other duties as assigned. Jim's support and encouragement enabled me to take the story of *La Belle* to many corners of Texas. The work of Alan Govenar will speak for itself as teachers use the films on the DVD included with this guide. I want to thank him for his persistence in moving this educational package to completion.

There were many teachers who taught about *La Belle* as it was being excavated. Their projects and interest in history encouraged me to create more and varied lessons. Many teachers will remain nameless. Those whom I know include educators from across the state. The staff at Somerville Middle School—Paula Harrison, lead teacher; Ann Shumate, principal, Kara Deal, Laura Simmons, Amy Bubela, Martha Hertenberger, Judy Brode, Denise Andruss, Jennifer Jordan, Lita Mann, and Bill Tune—taught an interdisciplinary unit for two years. Jim Kracht from TAMU facilitated their work. Regina Sanders at Dyess Elementary in Abilene developed a primary unit. Donnie Tegeler led a G/T project in La Ward. Cathey Sims shared her enthusiasm with seventh graders in Granbury. Carlita Kosty at Earl Rudder Middle School in San Antonio was one of several teachers whose students won recognition for History Fair projects based on *La Belle*. Jim Zuhn assisted with *Journeys*, the web site for educators. A teacher workshop sponsored by the Texas State Historical Association and facilitated by John Britt and Donna Britt introduced many teachers to concepts and lessons illustrated in the study of *La Belle*.

Museums and educators along the La Salle Odyssey trail continue each day to relate the story of La Salle. Visit them to see the artifacts: Corpus Christi Musuem of Science and History (Corpus Christi), Texas Maritime Museum (Rockport), Texana Museum (Edna), Calhoun County Museum (Port Lavaca),

Museum of the Coastal Bend (Victoria), Matagorda County Museum (Bay City), and Petite Belle Homeport (Palacios). The Texas State History Museum in Austin also hosts an excellent exhibit.

Thanks to Dylan Huntsman for the illustrations in Unit II.

Many people read the lessons included in this book and made suggestions. I want to thank the following teachers: Charis Smith (The Presbyterian School, Houston), Debra Hanus (Beeville ISD), and Kathy Huntsman (School of Excellence, San Antonio). I'm also grateful to the following education professionals: Carol Klages (UH Victoria), Marilyn Eisenwine (Angelo State University), Gayle Parenica (ESC Region 3, Victoria), and Brenda Whorton (educational consultant, Santa Fe).

Mary Lenn Dixon, editor in chief for Texas A&M University Press, encouraged the development of this book and moved the process forward.

As frequently happens with a project like this, my family learned more about La Salle and *La Belle* than they imagined possible. I thank them for their support and interest from the first time they visited the shipwreck and for their patience with the many hours of writing and editing: Jim, Carolyn, Kathy, Dylan, and Dede. And special thanks to my husband, Phil, who helped define the project and who rescued me often with his computer skills.

The discovery and investigation of *La Belle* was one of the most exciting archeological discoveries in recent times. It also illustrates history in the making; textbooks were rewritten, based on the findings. The world followed the progress of this unique excavation while multiple layers of artifacts and information were uncovered. Headlines ran in local, state, and national newspapers as patterns and artifacts related previously unknown details about the story of La Salle and his misadventure on the Texas coast. One *Houston Chronicle* byline read, "History rising from the bay's murky depths." The *Victoria Advocate* labeled the recovery of the first cannon, "CATCH OF THE CENTURY."

A dock attached to the cofferdam site encouraged people from all walks of life to join in the recovery effort. They came by small boats or charters and spent the day watching the detailed but intriguing work of the archeologists. It was one of the most public excavations ever, because the archeologists realized the importance and relevance of the investigation.

The sinking of this ship in 1686 literally changed the map of North America. It meant that the goals of the French to establish a stronghold on the Gulf of Mexico and challenge Spanish domination of the region were thwarted. Because of La Salle's physical presence on the Gulf coast the Spanish intensified their effort to expand and secure their territory, known as New Spain. The Spanish exerted their influence on the region and stayed.

As the story was unearthed, we learned more about explorers, colonists, and Native Americans. The Native Americans known as the Karankawa were at first hospitable. When the French blundered and took a canoe without permission, the Karankawa became hostile and a constant threat. The Caddo tribe, however, offered counsel as to the location of the Mississippi River and became active trading partners with the French. A little-known tribe, the Jumano, served as messengers and traders with the Spanish along the Rio Grande River and kept the Spanish informed of French activities.

Teachers and students followed the progress of the excavation over the Internet. Some students experienced the ultimate field trip—a day at the site watching the archeologists work. Students at one middle school devoted the entire year to a multidisciplinary study of *La Belle*. They became student experts on the project as cohorts from around the world contacted them for their perspective. Numerous history fair projects were inspired by the archeology of *La Belle*.

The story of *La Belle* offers a unique opportunity for students to become more involved in authentic learning. Students will learn to think like archeologists as they learn about the decades-long search for the wreck, study the unique excavation techniques and, finally, observe the pieces of the puzzle coming together. The hull of the ship has been conserved using a unique process and the artifacts are now in exhibits throughout the state of Texas.

This educational package will provide resources for teachers to guide their students, through research and technology, on an exciting journey. Resources include journal accounts of La Salle's expedition and the details of the archeological excavation found in *From A Watery Grave* (Bruseth and Turner). *The Shipwreck of* La Belle (Govenar) on DVD illustrates the operations of the excavation and *Dreams of Conquest* (Govenar), also on DVD, provides vivid insight into the life of La Salle and the work of historians.

This book provides four dynamic units for bringing students into the drama of this discovery. Teachers will likely choose single units or lessons to use. The first unit relates the many things students can learn from a shipwreck with specific examples from the excavation of *La Belle*. Unit Two is about the science of archeology, with hands-on activities that encourage students to experience the procedures used by archeologists. The third unit takes students around the world on the journeys of La Salle, and highlights mapping and sequencing skills. In Unit Four, students make connections with the cultures that interacted along the Gulf coast: French, Karankawa, Caddo, Spanish, and Jumano.

This study is easily integrated into many subject areas. Language Arts, Math, Science, Art, Technology, and Communication curriculum ideas will help teachers extend this material across the curriculum. Content knowledge enhances history, geography, economics, government, citizenship, and science. Skills such as critical thinking, problem solving, and decision making are woven into the lessons. This Study Guide will provide lessons for World History, Geography, United States History, and Texas History classes.

The time of La Salle was rich with adventure and intrigue. The court of Louis XIV and the society of France molded La Salle into an explorer and entrepreneur; the Spanish felt threatened by the incursion of another European power into the Gulf of Mexico; native Americans welcomed trade from Europe, yet defended their territory. The story is set on a world stage that illustrates the time and trials of exploration and colonization.

Join the inquiry that excited hundreds of teachers and students to learn through an archeological investigation. Experience with your students the fascinating story unearthed by the discovery of the shipwreck of *La Belle* and La Salle's adventures along the Texas Gulf Coast.

LA SALLE IN TEXAS

Overview

Unit Summary: Students will use information generated by the archeological studies of *La Belle* to create skits about the people associated with the ship.

ENDURING UNDERSTANDINGS

There are many ways to learn about the past.

Historians, archivists, and archeologists study the past to learn about how people lived.

Archeological discoveries are tools for learning about the past.

ESSENTIAL QUESTIONS

What can a shipwreck tell about the past?

How was a ship of exploration built in the 1600s?

How did sailors live (survive) aboard ships?

Was La Salle prepared for the expedition?

How might the United States be different if La Salle had succeeded in establishing a colony?

What would you do if you found a cannon or other old weapon?

SOCIAL STUDIES STRANDS — NATIONAL COUNCIL FOR SOCIAL STUDIES

Culture (French)

Production, Distribution, and Consumption (establishing a colony, setting up trade)

Science, Technology, and Society (excavation techniques, technology of 1600s)

Global Connections (politics of Europe in 1600s, implications if the colony succeeded)

Civic Ideals and Practices (stewardship of archeological sites)

CURRICULUM STANDARDS FOR SOCIAL STUDIES — NATIONAL COUNCIL FOR SOCIAL STUDIES

What happened in the past?

Why are things located where they are?

How do historic events influence regional and global settings?

How do people meet their basic needs in a variety of contexts?

What is the balance between rights and responsibilities of citizens?

How can students gain the skills to: acquire knowledge and manipulate data, construct new knowledge, work independently and cooperatively to accomplish goals?

TEKS:

4.1, 4.2, 4.6, 4.8, 4.9, 4.10, 4.11,
4.20, 4.22, 4.23, 4.24
5.1A, 5.6, 5.9, 5.10A, 5.11A, 5.25,
5.26, 5.27
6.2, 6.3, 6.7A, 6.8A, 6.14, 6.15,
6.16, 6.21, 6.22, 6.23
7.1, 7.2, 7.9, 7.16, 7.21, 7.22, 7.23
8.1, 8.2, 8.10, 8.11, 8.20, 8.24, 8.30,
8.31, 8.32

Getting Started

Level: grades 4–8
Subjects: social studies, science,
    math, computer technology, lan-
    guage arts, visual arts
Skills: critical thinking skills to or-
    ganize and use information ac-
    quired from a variety of sources,
    including electronic technology;
    communication skills for written,
    oral, and visual forms, problem-
    solving and decision-making
    skills, work skills (independently
    and with others in a variety of
    settings)
Time: 6 class periods 45–60 minutes
Class size: any number, divided into
    three or six groups for presenta-
    tion of 3 skits

RESOURCES FOR UNIT

Books
*Bruseth, James E. and Toni S.
    Turner, *From A Watery Grave:
    The Discovery and Excavation
    of La Salle's Shipwreck*, La Belle.
    College Station: Texas A&M Uni-
    versity Press, 2005. (referred to as
    FWG) Adult to intermediate level.
    A detailed account of the recovery

of *La Belle*. Many photographs
and illustrations. Some primary
accounts quoted. Excellent bibliography.

Audio Visuals
The Shipwreck of La Belle (Alan
Govenar). Documentary Arts and
La Sept Arte. 1998. DVD Detailed
account of the discovery, excavation, and laboratory procedures
used in recovering *La Belle*. First
person interviews with the archeologists and historians involved in
the project. *Please observe content
advisory for this DVD, p. 108. See
Guides to DVDs for detailed summary.*

Internet Connections — Using
Technology
www.thc.state.tx.us The Texas Historical Commission, preservation
agency for Texas. Provides photographs of the excavation and artifacts. Provides some timelines and
background information as well.
http://nautarch.tamu.edu Texas
A&M University, Nautical Archeology Program. Conservation
of *La Belle*. Offers many photographs of the artifacts as they are
being conserved.
www.tsha.utexas.edu/handbook/
online Handbook of Texas online.
Presents short articles and topics
related to *La Belle* and La Salle.
www.pbs.org/wgbh/nova/lasalle
Provides educational activities to
accompany the Nova video, *Voyage of Doom* 1999.
www.texasmaritimemuseum.org
Texas Maritime Museum (Rockport). Relates information about
the La Salle exhibit on display.

www.museumofthecoastalbend.org
Museum of the Coastal Bend
(Victoria). Offers some educational activities that complement
the exhibit on La Salle and especially Fort St. Louis.

MATERIALS AND EQUIPMENT
NEEDED

Projector for DVD
DVD, *The Shipwreck of* La Belle
Copies of INSTRUCTIONS FOR
    STUDENT GROUPS; one for
    each GROUP (6 groups)
Copies of student worksheets by
    groups, NOTES; copy for each
    student in each GROUP
Internet connections for using tech-
    nology
Materials to use for costumes of
    sailors, officers, and colonists (ex-
    amples: old jackets, large shirts,
    hats, cardboard, foil, etc.)
Bruseth, *From A Watery Grave*
    (FWG)
Copies of pages from *FWG* for use in
    groups: Group One, p. 66, Group
    Two, p. 75, Group Three, p. 85. (6
    groups)

Content Brief

BACKGROUND

Archeology is one way to learn about the past. Discoveries made by archeologists add information to the written record and often raise questions for historians, archivists, and other scholars to explore.

La Belle sank in Matagorda Bay in 1686 with a crew of sailors on board. The ship had been loaded with La Salle's possessions and made ready to sail when the Mississippi River's location was verified. The sailors had provisions for two weeks but were stranded for about three months.

When the ship was located in 1995 and later excavated, several interesting stories were revealed. First is the story of the construction of *La Belle* in France. *La Belle* was a "kit;" its timbers were numbered to make it easy to reconstruct. Research shows that La Salle intended to put the kit on another ship for the Atlantic crossing, then build it out to use in exploring the coast. However, La Salle needed *La Belle* as a transport, so it was assembled in France and sailed to the New World.

The second story is about how the sailors lived on the ship during the time they were stranded in Matagorda Bay. Bones found on *La Belle* indicate the sailors were eating bison, pig, duck, and goat. Empty casks likely contained water, wine, brandy, and flour. The aft cargo compartment was a jumbled mess, with cargo in disarray. It seemed that the barrels and crates had lined the sides of the compartment, but fell to the center when the ship ran

aground. Next, the sailors cleared the area to use for living quarters while they were stranded. They fashioned a brick-lined hearth. The human skeleton found in the bow on the coils of rope indicated that a sailor took refuge in the bow but died, separated from the others on the ship.

The third story tells how La Salle was prepared to sail on to the Mississippi River to establish an outpost. He loaded many provisions on *La Belle* to take with him. He left Joutel in charge of Fort St. Louis and went east to locate the Mississippi River. While he was gone, a storm wrecked *La Belle*. The stranded sailors lived on board until provisions ran out, then made a raft that carried them to Matagorda Peninsula. From there they found a canoe and paddled back to Fort St. Louis on Garcitas Creek.

From evidence found by the archeologists, we can create some fascinating scenes. Students will enjoy acting out the stories of (1) the construction of *La Belle* in France; (2) survival of the sailors on *La Belle* in Matagorda Bay; and (3) the outcome of the expedition debated by archeologists and historians.

VOCABULARY

Word bank for notebook or word wall for easy reference. Additional vocabulary is defined in the glossary.

Aft: rear section of a ship

Archeology (archaeology): the study of past cultures through their material remains

Artifact: an object that has been made or modified by humans

Bow: front section of the ship

Cargo: goods and weapons stored for transport

Cofferdam: watertight enclosure built in water, pumped dry to allow work inside

Hull: outer structure of a ship

Magnetometer: instrument for measuring presence of metal

UNIT STRUCTURE — W.H.E.R.E.

This unit structure will be used throughout the curriculum. The acronym **W.H.E.R.E.** stands for: Where is this lesson going; Hook students with interesting information; Explore the details and enable the student to learn; Reflect on new learning; Evaluate and assess student learning during the lesson.

WHERE

Students will learn what a shipwreck can tell about the past. Students will use information generated by archeological investigations to create short skits about events related to *La Belle* and answer the question: How might the United States be different if La Salle had succeeded in establishing a French colony?

HOOK

Class 1: Say to students: Archeologists work as detectives. Imagine that you came upon this scene (evidence that can be observed): (1) on the kitchen counter there is a cookie jar with the lid off, (2) on the front of your brother's shirt there are cookie crumbs. What conclusion might you infer from this observation?

Ask students: Can you think of another time that you could tell a story from evidence observed? What other examples can you give to illustrate the process of observation and inference?

Say to students: As we look at the work done by archeologists in Matagorda Bay, we will balance the evidence (observation) with conclusions (inference).

EXPLORE

Class 1: Use the INTRODUCTION to Unit One for all students (p. 5) and MAIN POINTS ABOUT THE SHIPWRECK OF *LA BELLE* (p. 5) to set the stage for the lesson.

Class 2: Review assignments from the INSTRUCTIONS FOR STUDENTS sheets for each GROUP (pp. 6, 8, and 13). Students will research and answer questions about their scenario. Students choose roles to research, assemble materials, assume characters, and create a skit.

Class 3 & 4: Groups continue to work on assignment.

Class 5: Groups will present short skit about their specific scenario.

Class 6: Continue skits by groups and all students write short essay to answer the question: How might the United States be different if La Salle had succeeded in establishing a French colony?

REFLECT

Students will write a short essay (5–10 sentences) to answer the question: How might the United States be different if La Salle had succeeded in establishing a French colony?

As a final discussion, students will answer: What would you do if you found a cannon or other old weapon?

EVALUATE

Rubrics provided under Standards section of Performance Tasks.

(group) Students will act out several scenes related to *La Belle*. Script, scenery, and costumes will enhance the presentations, but are not required.

(individual) Students will write a short essay answering the question: How might the United States be different if La Salle had succeeded in establishing a French colony?

Introduction to Unit One
for all students (Explore)

Essential questions, *posted* for students to consider:

- What can a shipwreck tell about the past?
- How might the United States be different if La Salle had succeeded in establishing a French colony?
- What would you do if you found a cannon or other old weapon?

Divide students into three or six groups, as needed, to develop skits about (1) the construction of *La Belle* in France; (2) survival of the sailors on *La Belle* in Matagorda Bay; and (3) the outcome of the expedition debated by archeologists and historians. Each skit has roles for 5 students.

Distribute INSTRUCTIONS FOR STUDENT GROUP for each group. Have groups review their INSTRUCTIONS sheet so they will take pertinent notes while they watch the DVD.

Introduce the story of *La Belle* by showing the DVD *The Shipwreck of* La Belle (54 min.; see Guide for DVDs, p. 107 to select specific chapters if viewing time needs to be shortened).

OR

Explain the discovery and excavation of *La Belle* by creating and showing transparencies from *FWG*, pp. 85 and 65 (see background information and other references) and a transparency of MAIN POINTS for discussion, below.

Remind students to take notes as they view the DVD presentation. They should read over the questions listed on the group's NOTES that will guide them.

MAIN POINTS ABOUT THE SHIPWRECK OF *LA BELLE*

- *La Belle* was constructed as a kit to be assembled in the New World. It was designed to sail in shallow waters for exploration. La Salle needed the ship for transport so it was built-out in France and sailed across the Atlantic Ocean. King Louis XIV helped finance the expedition because he was at war with Spain at the time and wanted to challenge Spanish control of the Gulf of Mexico.

- A crew of sailors lived on *La Belle* while La Salle traveled into East Texas looking for the Mississippi River. A storm in 1686 wrecked the ship and stranded the sailors until they built a raft. They got to Matagorda Peninsula, then found a canoe and paddled back to Fort St. Louis.

- La Salle loaded *La Belle* with his possessions to use to establish an outpost on the Mississippi River.

He then led a group into East Texas to locate the Mississippi River, planning to return for the supplies. While he was gone, *La Belle* was wrecked in the storm. When this happened, the colony lost many valuable supplies and lost contact with France. This event forced La Salle to begin a march to Canada.

FACETS OF UNDERSTANDING TO BE ANSWERED BY STUDENTS IN GROUPS AND AS AN ESSAY

Explanation: Describe what you can learn from a shipwreck.

Interpretation: How might the United States be different if La Salle had succeeded in establishing a French colony?

Application: What would you do if you found a cannon or other old weapon?

Perspective: Show how the La Salle expedition fits into historical context: What were European powers (France, England, Spain, Netherlands) doing at this time?

Empathy: Imagine how La Salle felt when he learned *La Belle* sank during the storm.

Self-knowledge: How would you feel if you were stranded? Compare the plight of the stranded sailors to a crew stranded in a space station.

Student Pages

La Salle in Texas,

UNIT ONE:

LEARNING

ABOUT THE

PAST FROM A

SHIPWRECK

Group One — France: Construction of La Belle

INSTRUCTIONS FOR STUDENT GROUP

Essential questions for students in GROUP ONE: See NOTES for worksheet.

FOR SKITS

How was a ship of exploration built? (*FWG* pp. 70–71, 75, 80) also see Macaulay, *Ship*

Who paid for *La Belle* to be built? Why? (*FWG*, pp. 19–20)

Why was *La Belle* built-out in France instead of being brought to the New World as a kit? (*FWG* p. 73–74)

FOR ESSAY

How might the United States be different if La Salle had succeeded in establishing a French colony?

FOR DISCUSSION

What would you do if you found a cannon or other old weapon?

FOR UNIT GOAL

What can a shipwreck tell about the past?

You will have two roles: one as researcher and one as a character in the skit.

Research Roles for students:

2 Research consultants: read *FWG* to answer questions and share information with group

2 Computer consultants: use Internet sites to answer questions and share information with group

1 Skit director: find materials for costumes and direct rehearsal of skit

CONSTRUCTION OF *LA BELLE* (skit)

Character Roles for skit:

Louis XIV: king of France

La Salle: explorer for France (will appear in two scenes)

Mallet: architect of plans for *La Belle*

Pierre: carpenter

Jacques: carpenter

Create conversations that give insight into the questions FOR SKITS posed above:

(1) between Louis XIV and La Salle about the king's support of the expedition (*FWG* pp. 19–20)

Plot: King Louis XIV is interested in securing territory in North America, therefore he supports La Salle's expedition.

(2) between La Salle and the architect, Mallet, about the size and purpose of the ship (*FWG* pp. 70–71)

Plot: La Salle wants a ship that can sail in shallow water along the coast.

(3) between the carpenters, Pierre and Jacques, about what wood to use (*FWG* p. 80) and how to number the timbers (*FWG* p. 78); also see Macaulay, *Ship*

Plot: Wood was scarce in France so timbers that were already cut were used. The *La Belle* was supposed to be put on another ship as a kit, then assembled when the expedition arrived in the New World.

References

From A Watery Grave (*FWG*) pages as listed above and copy of page 66.

Macaulay, *Ship* (how ships were built in the seventeenth century)

Internet Connections:

Using Technology

See "Stories in Timber" at www.pbs/org/wgbh/nova/lasalle/timber.

http://nautarch.tamu.edu. See project, *La Belle*, modeling

TIMELINE for reference

1670s: La Salle was in New France (Canada) seeking a route across the North American continent

1682: (April) La Salle claimed territory drained by Mississippi River for France, at the mouth of the river

1682: (October) Spain declared war on France

1683: La Salle visited Paris and King Louis XIV to get money, ships and supplies from the king

1684: (May & June) *La Belle* was constructed in Rochefort, France

1684: (July) *La Belle* sailed from La Rochelle

Name _____ Date _____

Group One – France: Construction of La Belle _____

NOTES

Take notes as you view the DVD and do research in books and on the
Internet so you can answer the following questions.

FOR SKIT

1. How was a ship of exploration built? (*FWG* pp. 70–71, 75, 80) also see
   Macaulay, *Ship*

2. Who paid for *La Belle* to be built? Why? (*FWG*, pp. 19–20)

3. Why was *La Belle* built-out instead of being brought to the New World
   as a kit? (*FWG* pp. 73–74)

FOR ESSAY

4. How might the United States be different if La Salle had succeeded in
   establishing a French colony?

FOR DISCUSSION

5. What would you do if you found a cannon or other old weapon?

FOR UNIT GOAL

6. What can a shipwreck tell about the past?

*La Salle in
Texas,*
UNIT ONE:
LEARNING
ABOUT THE
PAST FROM A
SHIPWRECK

Student Pages

La Salle in Texas,
UNIT ONE: LEARNING ABOUT THE PAST FROM A SHIPWRECK

INSTRUCTIONS FOR STUDENT GROUP

Essential questions for students in GROUP TWO. See NOTES for space to answer.

FOR SKITS
How did sailors live (survive) aboard ships?
Why was *La Belle* anchored in Matagorda Bay? (*FWG* p. 28)
Where did the sailors live on the ship? the livestock? (*FWG* p. 4, 6)
Were the Karankawa friendly or hostile? (*FWG* p. 4)

FOR ESSAY
How might the United States be different if La Salle had succeeded in establishing a colony?

FOR DISCUSSION
How would you feel if you were stranded as the sailors were? Compare the plight of the stranded sailors to a crew stranded in the space station.
What would you do if you found a cannon or other old weapon?

UNIT GOAL
What can a shipwreck tell about the past?

You will have two roles: one as researcher and one as a character in the skit.

Research Roles for Students:
2 Research consultants: read *FWG* to answer questions for skits (above) and share information.
2 Draftsmen: draw a diagram of *La Belle* to use as background or create an outline with tape or chalk to show the actual size. See chart below or *FWG*, p. 75.
1 Skit director: find materials for costumes and direct rehearsal of skit.

SURVIVAL OF SAILORS (Group Two skit)

Character Roles for skit:
JEAN: a sailor on *La Belle*
JOUTEL: second in command of expedition; in command at Fort St. Louis
CAPTAIN TESSIER: in charge of *La Belle* when the storm sank the ship
MICHEL: sailor on *La Belle* in Matagorda Bay when storm sank the ship
ANDRE: soldier/sailor on *La Belle* in Matagorda Bay when storm sank the ship
   (will appear in two scenes)

Create conversations that give insight into the questions FOR SKIT posed above.

(1) between Captain Tessier and Jean, a sailor, about going ashore to get fresh water (*FWG* p. 3–4)
Plot: Supplies were low because La Salle was gone longer than he thought.
(2) between Andre and Michel, sailors on *La Belle*, about the Karankawa Indians on shore (*FWG* p. 4)
Plot: Sailors worried about the Karankawa because some of the men angered the tribe by stealing their canoes.
(3) between Joutel and Andre when the soldier returns to Fort St. Louis (*FWG* p. 6)
Plot: Joutel, who was in charge of the fort, wondered what happened on *La Belle* during the storm.

References
From A Watery Grave (*FWG*) as listed above and copy of p. 75

Internet Connections
See www.thc.state.tx.us for details on La Salle project.

La Salle in Texas,

UNIT ONE:

LEARNING

ABOUT THE

PAST FROM A

SHIPWRECK

La Salle in Texas, UNIT ONE: LEARNING ABOUT THE PAST FROM A SHIPWRECK

CHART ABOUT WHERE THE SAILORS MIGHT LIVE
ON *LA BELLE* (also see *FWG*, p. 75; for Group Two skit)

Compartments	length	width	height	other
bow in hull	11 ft. 5 in.	12 ft.	7 ft.	rope, platforms for sleeping, hammock
main hold in hull	16 ft. 5 in.	14 ft.	7.5 ft.	hatch, cargo, locker with bilge pump
aft cargo hold in hull	10 ft.	12 ft.	7 ft.	hatch
lazarette in hull	9 ft.	12 ft.	5–7 ft.	hatch to cabin above, flammable materials
cabin on deck	6 ft.	12 ft.	5 ft.	had galley in front then captain's quarters

TIMELINE

1685: (October) La Salle gave list of provisions on *La Belle* to Joutel

1685: Twenty-seven men on board *La Belle* in northern part of Matagorda Bay

1685: provisions for two weeks — bones found in shipwreck: bison, pig, ducks, goat; casks for wine, brandy, flour, water

1685: five sailors in long boat go ashore to get water; don't return

1685: pulled anchor to drift nearer colony

1686: (January) storm beached *La Belle* in shallow water ¼ mile off shore; sailors built raft to sail to shore, drowned (author's note: few sailors could swim in 17th century)

(February) sailors built better raft and got to shore; offloaded some cargo and camped on Matagorda Peninsula

(April) six sailors returned to Fort St. Louis and related survivor stories to Joutel

DATA FROM ARCHEOLOGICAL INVESTIGATION (for Group Two skit)

Observation: Aft cargo compartment was a jumbled mess with cargo in disarray with a space cleared and lined with bricks to serve as a hearth. *FWG* p. 84
Inference: The sailors had cleared a space in the main hold to live — cook, eat, sleep — while they were stranded. Casks and barrels lined the sides of the hold but fell into center of cargo hold when the ship went aground.

Observation: Skeleton in bow on rope, empty cask nearby, porringer with "Barange" inscribed on it.
Inference: This sailor took refuge in bow but likely died quietly.

The archeologists used an electronic data system to record every artifact removed from the excavation. This allowed them to create a three-dimensional diagram of the cargo and ship's hull.

La Salle in Texas,

UNIT ONE:
LEARNING
ABOUT THE
PAST FROM A
SHIPWRECK

Name _____ Date _____

Group Two — Matagorda Bay: Survival of Sailors

NOTES

Take notes as you view the DVD and do research in books and on the internet so you can answer the following questions:

FOR SKITS
How did sailors live (survive) aboard ships?

Why was *La Belle* anchored in Matagorda Bay? (*FWG* p. 28)

Where did the sailors live on the ship? the livestock? (*FWG* p. 4, 6)

Were the Karankawa friendly or hostile? (*FWG* p. 4)

FOR ESSAY
How might the United States be different if La Salle had succeeded in establishing a colony?

FOR DISCUSSION
How would you feel if you were stranded as the sailors were? Compare the plight of the stranded sailors to a crew stranded in the space station.

What would you do if you found a cannon or other old weapon?

UNIT GOAL
What can a shipwreck tell about the past?

Group Three — Debate: Outcome of the Expedition

Student Pages

La Salle in Texas,

UNIT ONE:

LEARNING

ABOUT THE

PAST FROM A

SHIPWRECK

INSTRUCTIONS FOR STUDENT GROUP

Essential questions for students in GROUP THREE. See NOTES for space to answer.

FOR SKITS

What was packed on *La Belle*? (*FWG* pp. 85, 86–92)

Was the cargo on *La Belle* primarily for building a colony or for military purposes? (*FWG* pp. 85, 86–92)

Can you estimate the number of trade goods? (*FWG* pp. 85, 86–92)

Can you estimate the number of military supplies? (*FWG* pp. 85, 86–92)

Was La Salle well prepared for the expedition?

FOR ESSAY

How might the United States be different if La Salle had succeeded in establishing a colony?

FOR DISCUSSION

What would you do if you found a cannon or other old weapon?

UNIT GOAL

What can a shipwreck tell about the past?

You will have two roles: one as researcher and one as a character in the skit.

Research Roles for students:

2 Research consultants: read *FWG* to answer questions below and share information with group.

2 Video reviewers: review DVD for opinions of Bruseth and Gilmore.

1 Skit director: get materials for costumes and direct rehearsal of skit.

La Salle in Texas,

UNIT ONE: LEARNING ABOUT THE PAST FROM A SHIPWRECK

DEBATE: OUTCOME OF THE EXPEDITION (Group Three)

Characters Roles for skit:

La Salle: explorer in North America in 1600s

Joutel: second-in-command of expedition

Amy Green: archeologist, graduate student on project

Jim Bruseth: archeologist who was project director for *La Belle*, Texas Historical Commission

Kathleen Gilmore: archeologist who identified artifacts from Fort St. Louis in the 1950s

Bob Weddle: historian who wrote about La Salle

Create conversations that give insight into the questions FOR SKIT posed above

(1) between La Salle and Joutel about loading La Salle's goods on *La Belle* (*FWG* p. 28).

Plot: La Salle asked Joutel to load his personal baggage on *La Belle* and provisions to set up a new fort on the Mississippi River.

(2) between Bruseth and Green about the cargo and what it represents (CHPT. 8 in DVD) (*FWG* p. 140).

Plot: Bruseth and archeologist, Amy Green talk about the vast amount of trade goods found in the hold of *La Belle.*

(3) between Gilmore and Weddle about the loss of *La Belle* during the storm and its impact on the expedition (*FWG* p. 140).

Plot: Weddle believes that the loss of *La Belle* meant the ruin of La Salle since he could not easily get supplies or new people to reinforce the colony. Gilmore agrees.

References

From A Watery Grave (*FWG*) as listed above and copy of p. 85

DVD *The Shipwreck of* La Belle

TIMELINE

1684: (October) La Salle gave list of provisions to pack on *La Belle* to Joutel

1685: (January) Storm beached *La Belle* in shallow water ¼ mile off shore at Matagorda Peninsula; sailors built raft to sail to shore but drowned (author's note: few sailors could swim in 17th century).

(February) Sailors built better raft; offloaded some cargo and camped on Matagorda Peninsula

(April) Six sailors returned to Fort St. Louis and related survivor stories to Joutel

(May) La Salle returned to fort and learned that *La Belle* was wrecked.

1995: Cannon for *La Belle* is found by diver (THC); cofferdam is constructed; excavation begins. Complete in 1997.

Name _____ Date _____

Group Three — Debate: Outcome of the Expedition

NOTES

Take notes as you view the DVD and do research in books and on the Internet so you can answer the following questions.

FOR SKIT
1. What was packed on *La Belle*? (*FWG* pp. 85–92)

2. Was the cargo on *La Belle* primarily for building a colony or for military purposes? (*FWG* pp. 85, 86–92) Looking at the diagram of the cargo can you estimate the number of trade goods (beads, axes, etc.)? (*FWG* pp. 85, 86–92) Can you estimate the number of military supplies (cannon, shot, firepots, etc.)? (*FWG* pp. 85, 86–92)

3. Was La Salle well prepared for the expedition?

FOR ESSAY
4. How might the United States be different if La Salle had succeeded in establishing a colony?

FOR DISCUSSION
5. What would you do if you found a cannon or other old weapon?

UNIT GOAL
6. What can a shipwreck tell about the past?

Student Pages

La Salle in Texas,
UNIT ONE:
LEARNING
ABOUT THE
PAST FROM A
SHIPWRECK

La Salle in Texas,

UNIT ONE:

LEARNING ABOUT THE PAST FROM A SHIPWRECK

PERFORMANCE TASKS — G.R.A.S.P.S. (each group)
The acronym G.R.A.S.P.S. stands for **G**oal, **R**ole, **A**udience, **S**ituation, **P**roduct, **S**tandards that will be used throughout this curriculum.

Goal
Learn what the archeology of a shipwreck can tell us about the past.
(*Group*)
Create a skit about what archeologists learned by excavating the shipwreck of *La Belle.*
(*Individual*)
Write an essay that answers the question: How might the United States be different if La Salle had succeeded in establishing a colony?

Role
You will present a short skit about what the archeologists learned. You will be assigned a researcher role and also a character to portray in the skit.

Audience
Your class will learn about all three scenarios: (1) the construction of *La Belle* in France; (2) survival of the sailors on *La Belle* in Matagorda Bay; and (3) a debate by archeologists and historians about the outcome of the expedition.

Situation
Your skit will inform other students about your findings so that everyone will learn more about the shipwreck and the archeological investigations.

Product
(*Group*) You will create skits with conversations between historic characters. Minimal costumes and scenery may be brought to enhance the skit.
(*Individual*) Write a short essay (five to ten sentences) to answer this question: How might the United States be different today if La Salle had succeeded in establishing a colony?

Standards — Assessment
RUBRICS for Evaluation
Students may create the rubrics for themselves to be used as the scoring guide for assessment..

(*Group*) skit
Level 4 (highest): Three conversations between historic characters. Speakers project story clearly.

Level 3: Two conversations between historic characters. Speakers project story.

Level 2: One conversation between historic characters. Speakers are not easily heard.

Level 1: Little conversation between historic characters. Speakers have little to say.

(*Individual*) Short essay to answer question.

Level 4 (highest): Essay of five sentences or more — Develops ideas in very clear and logical way. Explains all ideas with facts and details. Uses excellent vocabulary, sentence structure with no errors in spelling, grammar, and punctuation.

Level 3: Essay of three sentences. Presents ideas reasonably well. Explains most ideas. Uses good vocabulary, sentence structure with few errors in spelling, grammar, and punctuation.

Level 2: Essay of two sentences. Reader has difficulty following the organization of ideas. Includes some facts and details. Includes some errors in spelling, grammar, and punctuation.

Level 1: One sentence. Essay lacks organization. Lacks supporting facts and details. Includes many errors in spelling, grammar, and punctuation.

Extend across the Curriculum

LANGUAGE ARTS

1) Write a journal entry as if you were one of the historical characters listed in the assignment.
2) Write and publish a newspaper or web site about the La Salle expedition.

CITIZENSHIP — ETHICS

1) Collectors: These mystery items were found on *La Belle*: Roman coin (*FWG* p. 110), fica (Spanish charm), (*FWG* p. 111), fossil (ammonite) (*FWG* p. 111) arrow point (Cuney type) (*FWG* p. 111–112)
How did these objects get on the ship? They seem to be out of place (without context). Were they objects that the sailors and officers collected? What will happen to artifacts that modern collectors leave in their garage or shoebox?
2) Pirates: Pirates were legendary in the seventeenth century. La Salle and his expedition encountered them several times. Do we have "pirates" in the twenty-first century? (Such as people who use public water sources without paying taxes or use fees, people who illegally copy Internet songs and movies)
3) Immigrants: Colonists who came to Texas with La Salle were planning a new life in a foreign country. What parallels do we have today? (graduate foreign students, green card workers, illegal immigrants, other)
4) Who owns sunken ships? There

is often debate between salvagers who locate the shipwreck and governments (nation or state) who claim ownership (*FWG* p. 72). www.pbs.org/wgbh/nova/lasalle/

ART/ LANGUAGE ARTS/ COMPUTER

1) Create a brochure or web site advertising the La Salle Odyssey, a trail of museums that displays the story and artifacts from *La Belle* and Fort St. Louis. Seven museums are part of the La Salle Odyssey:
Corpus Christi Museum of Science and History (Corpus Christi) www.ccmuseum.com
Texas Maritime Museum (Rockport) www.texasmaritimemuseum.org
Texana Museum (Edna, no web site available at time of writing)
Calhoun County Museum (Port Lavaca) www.calhouncountymuseum.org
Museum of the Coastal Bend (Victoria) www.museumofthecoastalbend.org
Matagorda County Museum (Bay City) www.matagordacountymuseum.org
La Petite Belle Homeport (Palacios) www.palaciosmuseum.org

MATH

1) Calculate the square foot space on the deck of the ship. Compare to space in classroom or on playground.
2) What does the "draft" of a ship mean? How deep is Matagorda Bay today? Could *La Belle* sail through Pass Cavallo into

Matagorda Bay today?
3) Study the geometry of shipbuilding. What does it take to float a boat?
4) Calculate the ocean pressure and predict its effect on the shipwreck under water.

SCIENCE

1) Experiment to see how a ship might sink. See Buoyancy Brainteasers www.pbs.org/wgbh/nova/lasalle/buoyancy.
2) *La Belle* was in an anaerobic environment after it sank. What does this mean? Develop and conduct experiments testing how fast objects decay in various environments.
3) Research and use navigational devices — past and present.
4) What are the ecological impacts of excavation — underwater and on land?
5) Research and analyze the diet of seventeenth century sailors and colonists. Compare it to your diet.
6) Learn about other famous shipwrecks such as *Mary Rose*, *Vasa*, and *Titanic* and compare their recoveries to that of *La Belle*.
7) Learn more about conservation of artifacts — especially wood and metal from underwater sites.

SOCIAL STUDIES/INTERNET

1) Use the La Salle story to participate in National History Day. Theme for 2007: Triumph and Tragedy in History and 2008: The Individual in History. See National History Day website for more details (www.nationalhistoryday.org/).

STUDENT NAME _____ DATE _____

1. The French explorer La Salle was part of a turning point in world history known as . . .

    A. Scientific revolution (ca. 1500–1700)
    B. Middle Ages (ca. A.D. 450–1450)
    C. Origin of civilization (ca. 3500 B.C.)
    D. Age of exploration and colonization (ca. 1450–1900)

Use the information in the box and your knowledge of social studies to answer question 2.

> Europeans explored the world.
> Europeans sought a trade route to Asia.
> Colonies were set up to gain wealth.
> Europeans tried to convert native peoples to Christianity.

2. What would be the best title for this information?

    A. Characteristics of the classical period
    B. Characteristics of the age of exploration and colonization
    C. Characteristics of the era of world wars
    D. Characteristics of the industrial revolution

Use the information in the box and your knowledge of social studies to answer question 3.

> Historians use written records.
> Cartographers use maps.
> Ethnographers use interviews.
> Archeologists use artifacts and patterns.

3. The best title for this information would be

    A. Ways to Learn about the Past
    B. Careers in Research
    C. Informative Sources
    D. Stories of the Past

4. The King of France, Louis XIV, partly financed La Salle's expedition because . . .

    A. he liked La Salle.
    B. he wanted to gain territory and challenge Spain.
    C. he wanted to visit the New World.
    D. he had many naval ships.

5. In order to find the mouth of the Mississippi River, La Salle sailed into the . . .

    A. Gulf of Mexico.
    B. Pacific Ocean.
    C. Bering Strait.
    D. Mediterranean Sea.

6. *La Belle* was designed to ...

    A. dive underwater.
    B. sail in shallow water.
    C. sail across the ocean.
    D. travel around the horn of Africa.

Use the diagram and your knowledge of social studies to answer question 7

murky water → importance of *La Belle* → ease of excavating → recovery of data → cofferdam built

7. Which is the best title for the diagram?

    A. Reasons for magnetometer survey in Matagorda Bay
    B. Reasons to dive in the Gulf of Mexico
    C. Reasons to search for shipwrecks
    D. Reasons to build a cofferdam around the wreck of *La Belle*

8. Bruseth writes in *From A Watery Grave*: "For want of a ship, Texas changed forever."

This statement refers to the fact that when *La Belle* sank . . .

    A. the French colony failed and the Spanish dominated.
    B. the native Indians gained territory.
    C. the French wished they had a ship.
    D. Texans can view exhibits about *La Belle*.

9. Use the information in the box and your knowledge of social studies to answer question 9

> He was born in France.
> He came to Texas in 1685.
> He was second-in-command at Fort St. Louis.
> He traveled to Canada after *La Belle* Sank.
> He wrote a journal about the La Salle expedition.

This best describes . . .

    A. Sieur de La Salle
    B. Henri Joutel
    C. Robert Weddle
    D. Pierre de Tessier

10. If I found a cannon or other old weapon, I would . . .

    A. sell it on the Internet.
    B. show it to my friends.
    C. hide it in my garage.
    D. report it to the state archeologist.

BE AN ARCHEOLOGIST: SIMULATED ACTIVITIES

Overview

Unit Summary: Students will conduct hands-on experiments to learn how archeologists work.

ENDURING UNDERSTANDINGS

There are many ways to learn about the past.

Historians, archivists, and archeologists study the past to learn about how people lived.

Archeological discoveries are tools for learning about the past.

ESSENTIAL QUESTIONS

How do archeologists work?

How does observation lead to inference?

What can students do to preserve the past?

SOCIAL STUDIES STRANDS — NATIONAL COUNCIL FOR SOCIAL STUDIES

Culture (French)

Production, Distribution, and Consumption (establishing a colony, setting up trade)

Science Technology and Society (excavation techniques, technology of 1600s)

Civic Ideals and Practices (stewardship of archeological sites)

CURRICULUM STANDARDS FOR SOCIAL STUDIES — NATIONAL COUNCIL FOR SOCIAL STUDIES

What happened in the past?

Why are things located where they are?

How do people meet their basic needs in a variety of contexts?

What is the balance between rights and responsibilities of citizens?

How can students gain the skills to:
Acquire knowledge and manipulate data,
Construct new knowledge,
Work independently and cooperatively to accomplish goals?

TEKS:

4.2, 4.6, 4.8, 4.9, 4.10, 4.11, 4.22, 4.23, 4.24

5.1, 5.6, 5.9, 5.10, 5.11, 5.25, 5.26, 5.27

6.2, 6.3, 6.7, 6.8, 6.14, 6.21, 6.22, 6.23

7.1, 7.2, 7.10, 7.16, 7.23, 7.24

8.1, 8.2, 8.10, 8.11, 8.20, 8.24, 8.30, 8.31, 8.32

Content Brief

The romance and mystery of archeology sparks the imagination of students and adults alike. Even before movies made pop stars of Indiana Jones and Lara Croft, the word "archeology" conjured up images of adventure. While we often think of archeology in exotic places, it is also in our own backyards.

This unit provides classroom lessons to simulate the methods used by archeologists. These lessons will give the students hands-on activities that simulate techniques used by researchers from the Texas Historical Commission on *La Belle*.

In this unit students will survey with a magnetometer, plot coordinates on a map, screen for artifacts, map cargo, classify artifacts, discover context, experiment with navigational instruments, and solve ethical dilemmas. Students will learn how archeologists use data and evidence to answer questions about how people lived in the past.

Each lesson in this unit generally stands alone and lasts one class period:
A. Graph the Results of a Magnetometer Survey
B. Dig Like An Archeologist
C. Map the Discoveries
D. Classify the Artifacts
E. Analyze Evidence
F. Draw Conclusions from Experiments with Hawk Bells
G. Recognize the Importance of Context
H. Experiment with Technology: Navigational Tools
I. Citizenship and Responsibility: Solve Archeological Dilemmas
J. Careers: Finding Opportunities

Before you begin these lessons, ask students to draw or sketch an archeologist. They should include the tools and setting in which the archeologist works. Save these papers for students to revise and enhance at the end of the unit to illustrate how much more they learned about archeologists.

Lesson A: Graph the Results of a Magnetometer Survey

OVERVIEW

Lesson Summary: Students will learn how a magnetometer works and how to plot coordinates on a map.

GETTING STARTED
Levels: grades 4–8
Subjects: social studies, science, visual arts, math
Skills: critical thinking skills to organize and use information; working independently and with others.
Time: 45–60 minute class period
Class size: any number of students divided into five groups for activity (OR one grid sheet per student)

RESOURCES
Books
Bruseth, *From A Watery Grave*

Audiovisuals
The Shipwreck of La Belle (DVD). *Please observe content advisory for this DVD, p. 108. See Guide to DVDs, p. 107 for detailed summary.*

Internet Connections—Using Technology
www.txarch.org/kids/lasalle A story by a student who visited the excavation of *La Belle*.
www.thc.state.tx.us The Texas Historical Commission, preservation agency for Texas. Provides photographs of the excavation and artifacts, timelines, and background information.
http://nautarch.tamu.edu Texas A&M University, Nautical Archeology Program, conservation of *La Belle*. Offers many photographs of the artifacts as they are being conserved.

MATERIALS AND EQUIPMENT NEEDED
copies of GRID FOR SURVEY RESULTS — 5 copies for 5 groups or 1 copy for each student
DVD *The Shipwreck of* La Belle
Projector for the DVD presentation
Overhead transparency of GRID FOR SURVEY RESULTS
Overhead projector
Access to Internet for further research

CONTENT BRIEF
When archeologists are looking for ships underwater, they survey with a magnetometer. This instrument rides on top of the water and detects metal, which shows up as an anomaly. The boat

pulling the magnetometer travels back and forth on imaginary grid lines to search for any anomaly, shown by an unusually high reading. After anomalies are plotted on a map, archeologists return to the location to dive and see what caused the high reading.

VOCABULARY

Word bank for notebook or word wall for easy reference. Additional vocabulary is defined in the glossary.

Anomaly: something abnormal; irregularity
Archeology (archaeology): the science that investigates the lives of people by studying their material remains
Coordinates: a set of numbers that locates a point in space in relation to a system of lines
Data: some facts or information
Grid: framework of parallel and crossed lines
Magnetometer: instrument for measuring magnetic forces

LESSON STRUCTURE: W.H.E.R.E.

Where is this lesson going; **H**ook students with interesting information; **E**xplore the details of the history and enable the student to learn; **R**eflect on new learning; **E**valuate and assess student learning during the lesson.

WHERE
Students will learn how a magnetometer works to show anomalies underwater and how to plot coordinates on a map.

HOOK
Ask students: How do archeologists find shipwrecks under water? Listen to several answers then suggest: Let's see what happened in 1995 in Matagorda Bay, Texas. Play CHPT. 1 from *The Shipwreck of* La Belle (DVD). This shows the boat pulling a magnetometer and divers locating the cannon from *La Belle.*

EXPLORE
After viewing the DVD *The Shipwreck of* La Belle, CHPT. 1, tell students they will plot results from an imaginary magnetometer. They will act as archeologists to record the data from a magnetometer as you call out the coordinates.

Distribute A GRID worksheet (one per group or one per student) for recording information.

Call out these coordinates to plot: A, 2: B, 2; C, 2; D, 2; E, 2; F, 2; G, 1¾; A, 2½; B, 2½; C, 2½; D, 2½; E, 2½; F, 2½; G, 2¾
Students should plot these coordinates then connect the dots to see what pattern they have. Add knobs at C, 2 and C, 2½; (bronze cannon — see photos *FWG* p. 43, 45, 85). Check to see how students did on this.

Dictate coordinates for a second object: draw dark line B, 4 to C, 4. Plot points C, 4; D, 4; E, 4; F, 4; C, 4¼; D, 4¼; E, 4¼; F, 4¼. Students should connect the dots to see an outline of this object (swivel gun — see outline on map plan *FWG*, p. 85)

REFLECT
What pattern comes on the grid sheet? (cannon and swivel gun)
What pattern would a WWII destroyer (all-metal hull) make? (solid shape of ship)

EVALUATE
If divided into groups, students work well together to accomplish the tasks.
Discuss or write: I would like (OR not like) to be an underwater archeologist because. . . .

La Salle in Texas,

UNIT TWO:

BE AN

ARCHEOLOGIST

Name _____ Date _____

Lesson A: A Grid for the Magnetometer Survey Results

This grid is ready for you to plot the coordinates located by the magnetometer. The lines are numbered and lettered. Mark a dot on each coordinate that was reported from the magnetometer.

A, 2; B, 2; C, 2; D, 2; E, 2; F, 2; G, 1¾; A, 2½; B, 2½; C, 2½; D, 2½; E, 2½; F, 2½; G, 2¾.

Connect the dots and see what you plotted. Add knobs at C, 2 and C, 2½.

Plot a second object with these coordinates

Draw dark line B, 4 to C, 4. Plot points C, 4; D, 4; E, 4; F, 4; C, 4¼; D, 4¼; E, 4¼; F, 4¼;

Connect the dots and see what pattern shows up.

scale: [_____] = 2 feet

Lesson B: Dig like an Archeologist

OVERVIEW

Lesson Summary: Students will test several techniques for recovering artifacts.

GETTING STARTED

Levels: grades 4–8

Subjects: science, social studies, math

Skills: critical thinking skills to organize and use information; problem-solving and decision-making skills, working with others in a variety of settings.

Time: preparation, 60 minutes; class, 45–60 minutes

Class size: students in two groups; 4 students in each group to act as "crew"

RESOURCES
Books
Bruseth, *From A Watery Grave*

Audiovisuals
The Shipwreck of La Belle (DVD)

Internet Connections — Using Technology
www.txarch.org/kids/lasalle
www.thc.state.tx.us The Texas Historical Commission, preservation agency for Texas. Provides photographs of the excavation and artifacts, timelines and background information.
http://nautarch.tamu.edu Texas A&M University, Nautical Archeology Program, conservation of *La Belle*. Offers many photographs of the artifacts as they are being conserved.

MATERIALS AND EQUIPMENT NEEDED

Transparency of DATA RECORDING SHEET

Copies of DATA RECODING SHEET — 2 for groups or 1 per student as an assignment

3 large sturdy plastic containers, approximately 24" x 36"

sediment: sand, gravel, small sea shells (do not use dirt)

artifacts (two sets, about 60 objects total): seed beads, bb's, jingle bells, toothpicks as substitute for straight pins, ceramic cups, plastic finger rings, other objects to simulate those found on *La Belle*

framed screen with ¼" mesh that will cover the top of the container 3

access to water

small plastic bags for artifacts

permanent marker for bags

blindfold for "diver"

trowel (archeologists most often use a 7" mason's trowel)

bucket

shop vac to remove water from container 2 OR quart container to dip out water

Preparation: (1) Fill containers 1 & 2 with sediment. (2) Place exactly the same artifacts into the sediment in containers 1 & 2. (3) Cover with 3 inches of water. Choose 4 students to serve as "crew" for each container (tasks listed in Explore). Remainder of class observe and take notes.

CONTENT BRIEF

BACKGROUND

When the shipwreck *La Belle* was identified there was much discussion about how to recover the cargo and hull. Some wanted to have divers use traditional underwater techniques. But the water was rarely clear enough for divers to see in order to lay out a grid and systematically remove artifacts. Others wanted to build a cofferdam around the ship, pump the water out of the dam, and excavate as if on land. The second method would be very expensive but lead to better recovery of the materials.

This demonstration will let students understand the differences in the procedures.

VOCABULARY

Word bank for notebook or word wall for easy reference. Additional vocabulary is defined in the glossary.

Artifact: any object made or modified by humans

Cofferdam: a water-tight enclosure

Grid: framework of parallel and crossed lines

Trowel: tool resembling a small, flat spade

Screen: (n.) a frame containing mesh; (v.) to press soil or shake through a screen and recover artifacts on top of screen

LESSON STRUCTURE: W.H.E.R.E.

Where is this lesson going; **H**ook students with interesting information; **E**xplore the details of the history and enable the student to learn; **R**eflect on new learning; **E**valuate and assess student learning during the lesson.

WHERE

Students will observe two procedures for recovering artifacts: (container 1) groping in murky water (called black water by divers) and (container 2) draining water from surface and troweling to remove sediment that is then screened to recover artifacts.

HOOK

Ask students: Have you ever waded at the beach and stepped on something you couldn't see? (Listen to several comments.)

When you reached down in the sand you pulled out a mystery object. Sometimes it broke because it was fragile. This can happen in underwater archeology if the water is murky and cloudy. Divers call these conditions "black water." This is a poor environment in which to recover artifacts. How could you clear up the water or recover the artifacts in these conditions?

Today we will conduct experiments that let you observe several techniques to recover the artifacts. Several students will serve as crewmembers to conduct the experiments and record the results.

EXPLORE

This experiment should be conducted outside, because it is messy. Choose two teams of 4 persons each; other students observe.

At container #1 — assemble a 4-person crew (diver who will be blindfolded, receiver to get artifacts, recorder to note what artifacts are recovered and how many, bagger to put artifacts into labeled bags).

At container #2 — assemble a 4-person crew (excavator who uses a trowel to remove the sediment and put it in a bucket, screener who dumps sediment on screen that is resting on container #3 and picks up artifacts to put them in labeled bags, recorder, and bagger).

Explain directions in advance so that both crews can begin work at the same time. They will have a defined time (5–10 minutes) to work.

At container #1, muddy the water by stirring the top sand into the water. The "diver" will be blindfolded and reach carefully into the sediment to pick out artifacts. Remind students there may be pointed objects in the mix. As the diver removes artifacts he hands them to the "receiver." The "recorder" makes notes on the data sheet and hands the artifacts to the "bagger" to put into the bag labeled "Container #1."

At container #2 have the "excavator" remove the water with the shop vac or quart container, then carefully dig out sediment and place it in the bucket. The "screener" dumps the bucket on the screen covering container #3. The sediment should go through the screen and leave artifacts for the "recorder" to note. The "bagger" will place the artifacts in bag labeled "Container #2."

Students will cluster around container #1 or container #2 to observe what artifacts are recovered and take notes on the DATA RECORDING SHEET.

REFLECT

At the end of 5–10 minutes, check to see what artifacts have been recovered. What observations can classmates make of the crews at work: ease of finding artifacts, speed with which they recovered materials, number of artifacts removed from sediment?

In the classroom have the "recorders" from each crew dictate information for the DATA RECORDING SHEET (transparency or student copies). Review the SHEET and questions with students or have them complete the SHEET as an assignment.

Ask the students: Can you determine which technique of recovery would give you the best information and why?

Show *The Shipwreck of La Belle* (DVD), chapters 1, 3, and 4 to confirm how the Texas Historical Commission investigated *La Belle*. Also see *FWG*, p. 39.

EVALUATE

Have students discuss or write a short answer to the question: If you have a chance to excavate a shipwreck, what techniques would you use to recover artifacts? Why?

Name _____ Date _____

Lesson B: Dig Like an Archeologist _____

DATA RECORDING SHEET

List the artifact types and record the number found in each dig.

Artifact types	Container 1 (from underwater)	Container 2 (from sediment)
Example — bells	2	4
Totals		

1. Which dig produced the most artifacts and why?

2. Which was the most effective dig and why?

3. If you have an opportunity to excavate a shipwreck, what techniques would you use to recover artifacts and patterns? Why?

Lesson C: Map the Discoveries

OVERVIEW

Lesson Summary: Students will learn how to plot coordinates on a map and interpret patterns.

GETTING STARTED

Levels: grades 4–8
Subjects: social studies, science, math
Skills: critical thinking skills to organize and use information; communication skills for written, oral and visual forms; problem-solving and decision-making skills, working independently and with others
Time: 45–60 minute class period
Class size: any

RESOURCES
Books
Bruseth, *From A Watery Grave*, pp. 85–92.

Audiovisuals
The Shipwreck of La Belle (DVD), chapters 6 & 7

Internet Connections—Using Technology
www.txarch.org/kids/lasalle
www.thc.state.tx.us The Texas Historical Commission, preservation agency for Texas. Provides photographs of the excavation and artifacts, timelines, and background information.
http://nautarch.tamu.edu Texas A&M University, Nautical Archeology Program, conservation of La Belle. Offers many photographs of the artifacts as they are being conserved.

MATERIALS AND EQUIPMENT NEEDED
Copies of worksheet GRID for MAP THE DISCOVERIES for each student
Transparency of GRID for MAP THE DISCOVERIES
Overhead projector
DVD *The Shipwreck of* La Belle
DVD projector

CONTENT BRIEF

BACKGROUND
Archeologists record their observations during excavation so they can recognize patterns formed by the artifacts. Mapping the artifacts is a useful way to record information. Sometimes two archeologists work together with one calling out the coordinates to the other who draws the artifacts on a map.

VOCABULARY
Word bank for notebook or word wall for easy reference. Additional vocabulary is defined in the glossary.

Artifact: any object made or modified by humans
Coordinate: a set of numbers that locates a point in space in relation to a system of lines
Grid: framework of parallel and crossed lines
Plot: to mark on a map

**LESSON STRUCTURE:
W.H.E.R.E.**

Where is this lesson going; **H**ook
students with interesting information; **E**xplore the details of the
history and enable the student
to learn; **R**eflect on new learning; **E**valuate and assess student
learning during the lesson.

WHERE
Students will plot artifacts on a grid
to see if they form a pattern.

HOOK
Say: If you looked at your dining
room table and saw (observed)
the table set with a cloth, napkins,
and flowers, you might guess (infer) that guests were coming for
dinner. You recognized a pattern
that told you what people (your
family) might do.
Today we will plot artifacts on a
grid like archeologists and see if
we can recognize a pattern (see
FWG, pp. 85–92).

EXPLORE
Give each student a copy of the
GRID for MAP THE DISCOV-
ERIES.
Say: You will be the "recorder" for

the excavation. When an artifact
is uncovered, it is plotted on the
grid by its coordinates. Sometimes one archeologist dictates
the coordinates to the recorder
to put on the grid map. You may
read and follow the instructions
on the grid map.

REFLECT
After students have drawn artifacts
on the grid map (10–15 minutes),
ask who recognizes a pattern (box
or crate with trade goods spilling
out of it).
Show chapters 6 and 7 from *The
Shipwreck of* La Belle, (DVD) or
FWG, p. 90.

You may preview the web sites of
THC and TAMU for more details
if you have the capability to project Internet sites for the students.

EVALUATE
Collect GRID for MAP THE DIS-
COVERIES to score.

Name _____ Date _____

La Salle in Texas,

UNIT TWO:
BE AN
ARCHEOLOGIST

Lesson C: Grid for Map the Discoveries

Draw lines from E, 2 to B, 3; from F, 3 to C, 4; from E, 2 to F, 3 and B, 3 to C, 4

Draw 5 Beads in unit F, 3; 8 Beads in E, 3

Draw 2 Combs in D, 3

Draw 4 Straight Pins in D, 4; 3 pins in C, 4

scale: [_____] = 9 inches

G

F

E

D

C

B

A

1   2   3   4

OBSERVATION
What patterns do you
see? _____

INFERENCE
How might this cargo be
used ? _____

Lesson D: Classify the Artifacts

OVERVIEW

Lesson Summary: Students will learn how archeologists classify artifacts to answer questions about how people might have used the cargo on *La Belle*.

GETTING STARTED

Levels: grades 4–8
Subjects: social studies, science, visual arts, math
Skills: critical thinking skills to organize and use information acquired from a variety of sources; communication skills for written, oral, and visual forms; problem-solving and decision-making skills, working independently and with others.
Time: 45–60 minute class period
Class size: any number, work in groups of 4 or 5

RESOURCES

Books
Bruseth, *From A Watery Grave*

Audiovisuals
The Shipwreck of La Belle

Internet Connection—Using Technology

www.txarch.org/kids/lasalle
www.thc.state.tx.us The Texas Historical Commission, preservation agency for Texas. Provides photographs of the excavation and artifacts, timelines and background information.
http://nautarch.tamu.edu Texas A&M University, Nautical Archeology Program, conservation of *La Belle*. Offers many photographs of the artifacts as they are being conserved.

MATERIALS AND EQUIPMENT NEEDED

ARTIFACTS sheet (one per group)
CLASSIFY THE ARTIFACTS worksheet (one per group)
Scissors to cut out artifacts (one pair per group)

CONTENT BRIEF

BACKGROUND

Archeologists want to learn about people and how they lived. To learn how people lived, archeologists develop a research plan that consists of a series of questions. These questions can be answered using archeological data.
Artifacts are classified to form part of the database.

VOCABULARY

Word bank for notebook or word wall for easy reference. Additional vocabulary is defined in the glossary.

Adzes: chisel-like tool, used as a wedge
Artifact: any object made or modified by humans
Attributes: a characteristic that can be assigned to a thing
Classify: to arrange in a set or group according to common attributes
Crucifix: cross with Christ figure on it
Data: facts, information
Muskets: guns of the 16th and 17th century; ignited by flint spark on powder
Pewter: metal alloy of tin and lead
Pipe: long stemmed pottery pipe for smoking tobacco
Shot: iron balls, vary in size from b-b to cannon balls, used in cannon and muskets
Signet: small seal used to make an impression on documents

LESSON STRUCTURE: W.H.E.R.E.

Where is this lesson going; **H**ook students with interesting information; **E**xplore the details of the history and enable the student to learn; **R**eflect on new learning; **E**valuate and assess student learning during the lesson.

WHERE

Students will sort and classify artifacts from *La Belle* to answer questions about the people and how they might have used the cargo.

HOOK

Have you ever grouped objects (such as toys, clothes, foods) together? Why did you do that? (to organize for use and ease of locating, i.e. all socks in one drawer) This system of organization is called "classification."

EXPLORE

Say: We are going to see how archeologists use grouping or classification to answer questions about the behavior of people.

You are a team of archeologists who has completed the excavation of *La Belle*. You are ready to begin analyzing the artifacts in the lab to learn about the people who were on the expedition. You will use these questions to classify the artifacts by function.

Question 1. What could they use for defense?

Question 2. What could they trade with the Native Americans they encountered?

Question 3. Describe the artifacts that were used by the crew personally.

Question 4. List the artifacts that might be used to set up a house.

Question 5. What category is missing? Write your own question here.

Distribute an ARTIFACTS sheet and a pair of scissors to each group and a CLASSIFY THE ARTIFACTS worksheet to each group.

Have them cut out the artifact cards to use in answering the questions on the CLASSIFY THE ARTIFACTS sheet.

Students will sort (classify) the artifacts to answer each question in turn. Some artifacts may go in more than one category.

Ask students to create their own questions (#5 on worksheet) and classify the artifacts to answer that question.

REFLECT

Review answers on CLASSIFY ARTIFACTS worksheets.

Question 1. Iron shot, gunpowder, muskets, fire pots, bronze cannon.

Question 2. Iron axe heads, glass beads, iron chisels, brass finger rings, iron needles, iron adzes, wooden combs, brass bells, brass pins.

Question 3. Wooden crucifix, wooden comb, ceramic pipe, ceramic cup, game pieces, brass signet.

Question 4. Iron axe heads, iron chisels, grinding stone, pewter plates, copper kettles, ceramic cup, brass candlesticks, pewter cup.

Ask what questions students added (#5 on worksheet).

To reinforce the concept of learning about behavior from artifacts and patterns, ask what an archeologist might find if you walked away from your birthday party without cleaning up. Do you think an archeologist could recognize the event?

EVALUATE

Collect and score the CLASSIFY ARTIFACTS worksheets.

Cut these artifact cards apart to use with CLASSIFY THE ARTIFACTS worksheet.

Wooden crucifix	Iron shot	Barrel—gunpowder	Iron axe head
Glass beads	Iron chisel	Musket	Brass finger rings
Ceramic fire pot	Grinding stone	Bronze cannon	Iron needles
Iron adze	Pewter plates	Ceramic pipe	Wooden comb
Copper kettles	Ceramic cup	Brass signet	Brass bells
Brass candlestick	Pewter cup	Game pieces	Brass pins

Illustrations by
Dylan Huntsman

Student Pages

La Salle in Texas,
UNIT 2:
BE AN ARCHEOLOGIST

Name _____ Date _____

Lesson D: Classify the Artifacts

Classify the artifacts from *La Belle* into groups that answer the following questions:

Question 1. What could they use for defense?

Question 2. What could they trade with the Native Americans they encountered?

Question 3. Describe the artifacts that were used by the crew personally.

Question 4. List the artifacts that might be used to set up a house.

Question 5. (your question)_____

Lesson E: Analyze the Evidence

OVERVIEW
Lesson Summary: The students will view artifact cards to make observations, then inferences.

GETTING STARTED

Levels: grades 4–8

Subjects: social studies, science, language arts, visual arts

Skills: critical thinking skills to organize and use information acquired from a variety of sources; communication skills for written and visual forms; problem-solving and decision-making skills, working independently.

Time: 45–60 minute class period

Class size: any number, divide into 4 or 8 groups, or each can work individually

RESOURCES
Books

Bruseth, *From A Watery Grave*, pp. 83, 89, 108

Internet Connections — Using Technology

www.thc.state.tx.us The Texas Historical Commission, preservation agency for Texas. Provides photographs of the excavation and artifacts. Some timelines and background information as well.

http://nautarch.tamu.edu Texas A&M University, Nautical Archeology Program, conservation of *La Belle*. Offers many photographs of the artifacts as they are being conserved.

MATERIALS AND EQUIPMENT NEEDED

Artifacts cards (four per sheet, cut apart) — one card per group or one card per student

Record Sheet — one per group or one per student

Rulers with metric markings

Objects to replicate the artifacts: protractor for drawing circles, spout from glue bottle, copper wire, jingle bell

CONTENT BRIEF

Archeologists analyze artifacts to tell about the lives of people. Four artifacts were selected from those brought to the surface in 1995 from *La Belle*. Archeologists made these artifact drawings (actual size) in the field. The numbers on the illustrations have meaning. 41 MG 86 is the archeological site number. 41 stands for the state of Texas, MG for Matagorda County and 86 for the 86th site recorded in the county. Each artifact then has an individual number. 00784 is a pair of dividers. They were navigational instruments used to calculate distance on a map. 00770 is two views of the tip of a powder horn. This worked as a spout for pouring gunpowder into a musket or cannon. 00760 is a hook used to suspend a pot over a cooking fire. 00759 is two views of a hawking bell. These were used in Europe in falconry. In the New World they were traded to Native Americans who used them as decorations.

VOCABULARY

Word bank for notebook or word wall for easy reference. Additional vocabulary is defined in the glossary.

Dividers: instrument used for navigation as compass (protractor)

Hawking bell: brass bell attached to a falcon's leg to sound its location (similar to jingle bell)

Inference: derived by reasoning; conclusion drawn from evidence

Observation: taking note; paying attention

Powder flask: container used for gunpowder

Action plan

LESSON STRUCTURE: W.H.E.R.E.

Where is this lesson going; **H**ook students with interesting information; **E**xplore the details of the history and enable the student to learn; **R**eflect on new learning; **E**valuate and assess student learning during the lesson.

WHERE
The students will view artifact cards that show objects removed from *La Belle*. They will make observations, then inferences.

HOOK
Give one artifact card to each group or each student. Tell them they came from the 1995 testing for *La Belle*. Ask if they can guess what they are.

EXPLORE
Show the objects that replicate the artifacts as hints (protractor, jingle bell, spout to glue bottle, wire). After some discussion, explain what the artifacts are.

Say: When archeologists find artifacts, they sketch and write everything about them in the records and reports. Complete the RECORD SHEET by taking measurements and describing the artifacts.

REFLECT
The artifacts were chosen to enable teachers to extend the discussion.
00784 dividers: navigation and mapping
00770 tip for flask of gunpowder: weapons and defense
00760 hook for cook pot: daily needs for food, clothing, and shelter
00759 hawking bell: items for trade with Native Americans

Have students make drawings showing the use of the artifacts by the French: a scene in which the object is used.

EVALUATE
Collect and score the RECORD SHEET.

41 MG 86
#00784
Bronze

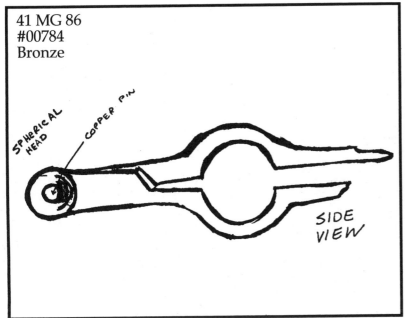

41 MG 86
#00770
Bronze

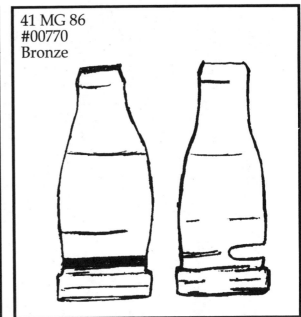

41 MG 86
#00760
Copper

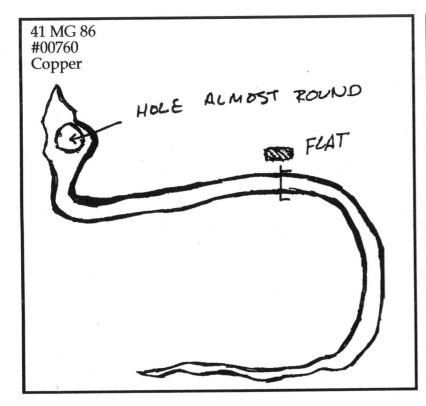

41 MG 86
#00759
Brass

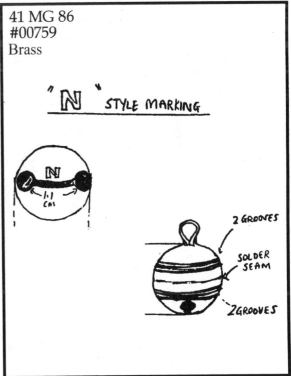

Student Pages

La Salle in Texas,

UNIT TWO:

BE AN

ARCHEOLOGIST

Name _____ Date _____

Lesson E: Analyze the Evidence

RECORD SHEET

Site # _____ Artifact #_____

OBSERVATION   SKETCH OR DRAWING OF ARTIFACT

Description: _____

Material: _____

Size: length _____

         width _____

Shape: _____

Color: _____

Other: _____

INFERENCE

Look for clues that tell you more about the artifact than you can directly observe. What does it tell us about human behavior?

What was its function (use)? _____

Where was it used (location)? _____

How was it made (manufactured)?_____

What technology was needed to make it? _____

Where was it made? _____

What other inferences can you make about the people who used this artifact?

_____

Draw a scene with people using one of the artifacts (on the back).

Lesson F: Draw Conclusions from Experiments with Hawk Bells

OVERVIEW

Lesson Summary: Students will experiment to test a theory (hypothesis) about hawk bells.

GETTING STARTED

Levels: grades 4–8
Subjects: science, math, social studies, language arts
Skills: critical thinking skills to organize and use information; communication skills; problem-solving and decision-making skills, working independently
Time: 45–60 minute class period
Class size: any number, students in pairs, space to do experiment outside

RESOURCES
Books
Bruseth, *From A Watery Grave*, p. 83

Audiovisuals
The Shipwreck of La Belle (DVD)

Internet Connections — Using Technology
www.thc.state.tx.us The Texas Historical Commission, preservation agency for Texas. Provides photographs of the excavation and artifacts, timelines and background information.
http://nautarch.tamu.edu Texas A&M University, Nautical Archeology Program, conservation of *La Belle*. Offers many photographs of the artifacts as they are being conserved.

MATERIALS AND EQUIPMENT NEEDED
Photograph of hawk bells *FWG* p. 83
5 jingle bells of different size or different materials per group (see importance of this in Explore)
1 tape measure per group to establish distance
1 copy of DRAW CONCLUSIONS worksheet for each pair of students

CONTENT BRIEF

Brass bells, similar to jingle bells, were part of the cargo in *La Belle*. When the archeologists saw the small bells, they recognized them as hawk bells (hawking bells).
In Europe these bells were used for falconry, a popular sport where trained falcons competed to kill and return with prey. Two bells of different pitches were tied to the falcon's foot so the trainer could locate his falcon as it flew after game (rabbits, mice, etc.).
In North America the bells were popular trade items that the Native Americans used as decorations on clothing. The Native Americans had few items made of metal before the European traders came.

LESSON STRUCTURE: W.H.E.R.E.

Where is this lesson going; **H**ook students with interesting information; **E**xplore the details of the history and enable the student to learn; **R**eflect on new learning; **E**valuate and assess student learning during the lesson.

WHERE

Students will experiment to test the explanation of why two bells of different pitches were tied together.

HOOK

It is reported that two bells of different pitches were paired and attached to the falcon so it could be heard farther away than with one bell alone.

EXPLORE

Say to students: develop an experiment to prove or disprove this theory.

You will need (A) one jingle bell, (B) two jingle bells of the same pitch and (C) two jingle bells with different pitches.

Have a partner take the bells and walk five meters away, then ring the bells — different combinations in a random order that you don't know (your partner should note what bells he rings for the different trials: A, B, or C).

Record (1 lowest, 10 highest) the intensity of the sounds for the different trials (A, B, or C).

Have your partner try different distances to see how far away you can hear the bells in the three different combinations.

REFLECT

What is your conclusion?

EVALUATE

Review student notes for consistency.

Name _____ Date _____

Lesson F: Draw Conclusions from Experiments with Hawk Bells

La Salle in Texas,
UNIT TWO:
BE AN
ARCHEOLOGIST

Have a partner take the bells and walk five meters away then ring the bells — different combinations in a random order that you don't know: (A) one bell alone, (B) two bells with same pitch, (C) two bells with different pitches (your partner should note the order in which he rings the bells for the different trials — A, B, or C).

Record (1 lowest, 10 highest) the intensity of the sounds for the different trials (A, B, or C).

Have your partner try different distances to see how far away you can hear the bells.

CAN YOU HEAR DIFFERENT PITCHES FROM A DISTANCE?

Distance from bells	Loudness 1–10 (10 loudest)
Five meters (5m)	
A	
B	
C	
_____ meters (fill in distance)	
D	
E	
F	
CONCLUSION	

After you have listened to all three combinations (A, B, and C), you and your partner should compare your answers to how he/she set up the experiment. What combination of bells did he/she ring, and in which order? Which ones were easiest to hear, and which ones were most difficult? Develop a concluding statement.

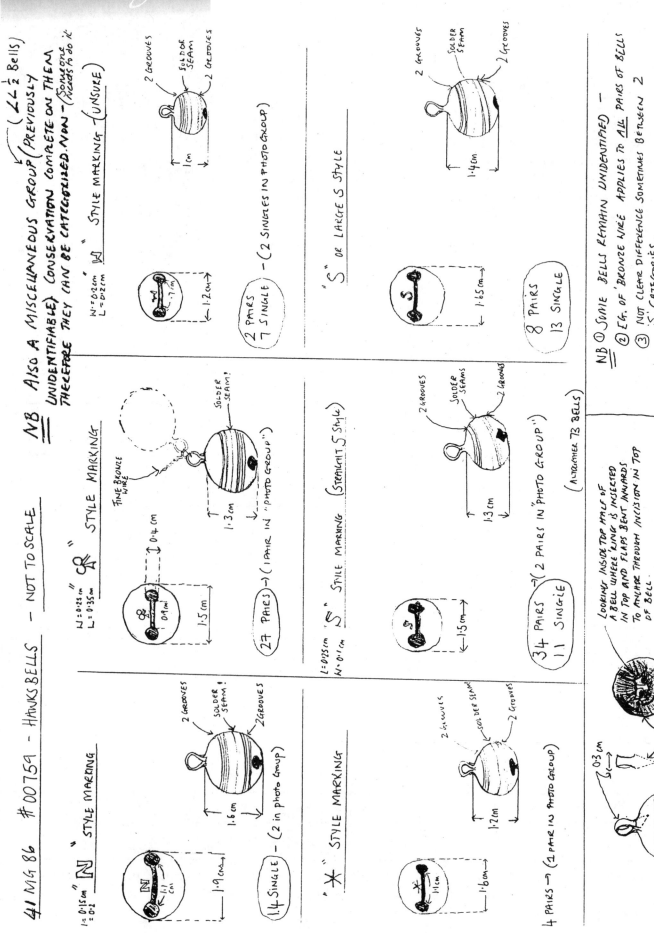

41 MG 86   #00759 - HAWKS BELLS   - NOT TO SCALE

NB Also a Miscellaneous group (previously unidentifiable) conservation complete on them therefore they can be categorized. Now - (someone needs to do it)   (< < ½ Bells)

"N" STYLE MARKING
1 = 0·15cm
= 0·2

L = 1·1 cm

1·9 cm

1 SINGLE - (2 in photo group)

"✳" STYLE MARKING
L = 0·25 cm
N = 0·1 cm

"S" STYLE MARKING (STRAIGHT S Style)

1·5 cm

1·1cm

4 PAIRS → (1 PAIR IN PHOTO GROUP)

2 GROOVES   SOLDER SEAM!   2 GROOVES
1·6 cm
1·2 cm

"⋇" STYLE MARKING
L = 0·25 cm
L = 0·35 cm
0·4 cm
0·9 cm
1·5 cm

FINE BRONZE WIRE
SOLDER SEAM!
1·3 cm

27 PAIRS → (1 PAIR IN "PHOTO GROUP")

2 GROOVES   SOLDER SEAMS   2 GROOVES
1·3 cm

34 PAIRS
11 SINGLE   (2 PAIRS IN "PHOTO GROUP")

(ALTOGETHER 73 BELLS)

LOOKING INSIDE TOP HALF OF A BELL WHERE 'RING' IS INSERTED IN TOP AND FLAPS BENT INNARDS TO ANCHOR THROUGH INCISION IN TOP OF BELL.
0·3 cm

"W" STYLE MARKING (UNSURE)
N = 0·2cm
L = 0·2cm
1·7m
1·2 cm

2 GROOVES   SOLDER SEAM   2 GROOVES
1 cm

2 PAIRS
7 SINGLE   - (2 SINGLES IN PHOTO GROUP)

"S" or LARGE S STYLE
1·65 cm

2 GROOVES   SOLDER SEAM   2 GROOVES
1·4 cm

8 PAIRS
13 SINGLE

NB ① Some bells remain unidentified —
② Eg. of 'Bronze wire' applies to all pairs of bells
③ Not clear difference sometimes between 2 'S' categories.

Lesson G: Recognize the Importance of Context

OVERVIEW

Lesson Summary: Students will understand the importance of context (association) of artifacts.

GETTING STARTED

Levels: grades 4–8
Subjects: social studies, science, language arts, visual arts
Skills: critical thinking skills to organize and use information; communication skills; problem-solving and decision-making skills; working independently
Time: 45–60 minute class period
Class size: any number

RESOURCES
Books
Bruseth, *From A Watery Grave*, p. 86

Audiovisuals
The Shipwreck of La Belle (DVD)

Internet Connections—Using Technology
www.txarch.org/kids/lasalle
www.thc.state.tx.us The Texas Historical Commission, preservation agency for Texas. Provides photographs of the excavation and artifacts, timelines and background information.
http://nautarch.tamu.edu Texas A&M University, Nautical Archeology Program, conservation of *La Belle*. Offers many photographs of the artifacts as they are being conserved.

MATERIALS AND EQUIPMENT NEEDED
Transparency of map of lazarette area in *La Belle* from sketch notes provided, p. 47.
Photograph of a firepot (*FWG* p. 86).

CONTENT BRIEF

Context is a very important concept for archeologists. "Context" means the surrounding environment that gives more meaning to individual artifacts. Artifacts have more meaning in association with other artifacts or features.

On *La Belle*, archeologists didn't recognize the ceramic vessels they found in the lazarette, a small hold in the stern, entered through the captain's quarters. Each pot had several handles and a lid. Inside were metal grenades. These objects were firepots, weapons that were thrown at enemy ships. They were designed to explode and cause damage to an enemy.

Their context was also important. They were located all together in a stern hold. They were ready for use but also protected from accidentally misfiring.

VOCABULARY
Word bank for notebook or word wall for easy reference. Additional vocabulary is defined in the glossary.

Context: surrounding environment, association
Firepot: ceramic vessel filled with flammable material and a grenade, something like a Molotov cocktail
Lazarette: stern hold

Action Plan

LESSON STRUCTURE: W.H.E.R.E.

Where is this lesson going; Hook students with interesting information; Explore the details of the history and enable the student to learn; Reflect on new learning; Evaluate student learning during the lesson.

WHERE
Students will relate items of importance (artifacts) from their bedrooms, view context of artifacts on *La Belle*, and plan a time capsule.

HOOK
Visualize your bedroom at home. List 10 items that tell something about you: family, friends, sports, pets, etc. All of these things together give a snapshot of you. If something were removed the picture would be incomplete.

EXPLORE
Show the map of the lazarette area of *La Belle* — (archeologist's drawing, description (*FWG*, p.71) and a photograph of the firepot (*FWG*, p. 86).
Say: Looking at the archeologist's notes, can you tell what compartment of the ship is represented?

REFLECT
Why were all the firepots in one location? (in case of accidental explosion, the fire and damage might be contained)

EVALUATE
What 10 items (artifacts) would you put in a time capsule that would tell about you in 100 years?

Unit Sub-Datum SW Corner   −25 cm   Mapping Point ⊖
PROJECT: 41MG86   DATE: 06 / NOV /1996   EXCV BY: C. Meide   SCALE: /cm : 5cm/

GRID SQUARE: 2010   N/ 2669 E   BW: ✓   ROLL: 24   EXP(S): 06

EXCV LEVEL: 0-10 (Northern quads) 0-40 (South)COLOR: ✓   ROLL: 24   EXP(S): 01 ; Roll 25 Fr 36, 35

MUNSELL COLOR: _____
COMMENTS: concentration of birdshot / standard size shot   B — Ballast   • — Gunflint   c — concretion   Wood (hull, cask)   Bone

CKD BY: TLC   DATE: 11 / 18 /1996   PAGE 1 of 2

Lesson H: Experiment with Technology: Navigational Tools

OVERVIEW

Lesson Summary: Students will experiment with an astrolabe to understand the difficulties of navigation in the 1600s.

GETTING STARTED

Levels: grades 4–8
Subjects: social studies, science, technology, visual arts, math
Skills: critical thinking skills to organize and use information; problem-solving and decision-making skills; working independently in a variety of settings.
Time: 45–60 minute class period
Class size: any number, in groups of 4 or 5 students

RESOURCES
Books

Bruseth, *From A Watery Grave*, pp. 109–110 (nocturnal and other instruments for navigation)

Internet Connections — Using Technology

www.thc.state.tx.us The Texas Historical Commission, preservation agency for Texas. Provides photographs of the excavation and artifacts, timelines and background information.
http://nautarch.tamu.edu
Texas A&M University, Nautical Archeology Program, conservation of *La Belle*. Offers many photographs of the artifacts as they are being conserved.

MATERIALS AND EQUIPMENT NEEDED

For each group:
1 protractor
1 drinking straw
1 fishing weight or other type of weight
transparent tape
string (12")
baggie for astrolabe to be sent home for night time experiment

CONTENT BRIEF

An astrolabe is a medieval instrument, later replaced by the sextant, used to determine the altitude of celestial bodies in the sky. Latitude may be determined in the Northern Hemisphere by the altitude of Polaris (the North Star). Sailors used celestial navigation to determine their latitude.

VOCABULARY

Word bank for notebook or word wall for easy reference. Additional vocabulary is defined in the glossary.

Astrolabe: an instrument formerly used for taking altitude of the stars at sea, now superceded by the quadrant and sextant
Altitude: measure of elevation
Latitude: distance north or south of the equator
Longitude: distance east or west of the prime meridian (Greenwich, England)
Polaris: a star located at the tip of the handle of the Little Dipper, the North Star; star at which the earth's axis points; the only star in the sky that doesn't appear to move with the earth's rotation

LESSON STRUCTURE: W.H.E.R.E.

Where is this lesson going; **H**ook students with interesting information; **E**xplore the details of the history and enable the student to learn; **R**eflect on new learning; **E**valuate and assess student learning during the lesson.

WHERE

Students will build and use an astrolabe to determine latitude. This must be done on a clear night.

HOOK

Have you ever used a compass to determine direction? What can a compass tell you? (the direction of the North Pole) What instrument can tell you where you are? (With an astrolabe or sextant you can tell latitude. You also need to know longitude to establish the point where you are.)

EXPLORE

You can assemble an astrolabe using the supplies in front of you. Then you can use it on a clear night.

1) Directions for making the astrolabe.
Tape the drinking straw to the protractor so that the straw lies exactly across the center of the protractor and the 90 degree mark.
Thread the string through the hole in the center of the protractor and tie it around the straw. Tie the other end of the string to the fishing weight. Let it hang freely.

2) Use your astrolabe to measure latitude.
On a clear night, look in the northern sky for Polaris, often called the North Star. Spot Polaris through the drinking straw. Hold it until the string stops swinging. Then press the string against the protractor and hold it in that position. The string will cross the protractor, showing a number of degrees: that is your latitude. You should repeat this measurement several times and use an average.
Locate an atlas or map on the Internet and check your latitude. Did you calculate that same latitude when you sighted the North Star with your astrolabe?

REFLECT

To know where you are located you must have two coordinates: latitude and longitude. To calculate longitude you must know how many hours you have traveled and how fast you are moving. A timepiece that could travel across oceans was not invented until 1745. In 1684, La Salle could not accurately calculate longitude.
Do you think La Salle would have found the Mississippi River from the Gulf of Mexico if he could have calculated his longitude? Why or why not?

EVALUATE

How closely did the students' readings register to the actual latitude for your location?

Lesson I: Citizenship and Responsibility: Archeological Dilemmas

OVERVIEW

Lesson Summary: Students will review and dramatize archeological dilemmas.

GETTING STARTED

Levels: grades 4–8
Subjects: social studies, science, language arts
Skills: critical thinking skills to organize and use information; communication skills; problem-solving and decision-making skills; working with others
Time: 45–60 minute class period
Class size: any number, divided into six (6) groups

RESOURCES
Books
Bruseth, *From A Watery Grave*, pp. 47–48.

Internet Connections — Using Technology
www.thc.state.tx.us The Texas Historical Commission, preservation agency for Texas. Provides information on Antiquities Code.
www.saa.org Society for American Archeology. See code of ethics.

MATERIALS AND EQUIPMENT NEEDED
Copy of one SCENARIO CARD for each group
Blank paper (8 ½ x 11) for each student
Markers of colors for drawing — one set per group
Additional information about archeological ethics (see www.saa.org)

CONTENT BRIEF

Every year many archeological sites are lost (damaged or destroyed) due to vandalism, construction projects and uninformed collecting. Currently laws protect archeological sites and artifacts only on public land. When vandalism is noticed on public land, officials should be called. On most private land, the owner controls what happens.

VOCABULARY

Word bank for notebook or word wall for easy reference. Additional vocabulary is defined in the glossary.

Dilemma: a situation requiring a choice between equally objectionable alternatives
Ethics: rules of conduct
Vandalism: willful destruction of property

**LESSON STRUCTURE:
W.H.E.R.E.**

Where is this lesson going; **H**ook students with interesting information; **E**xplore the details of the history and enable the student to learn; **R**eflect on new learning; **E**valuate and assess student learning during the lesson.

WHERE
Students will review scenarios where archeological sites are being disturbed (problem), and suggest actions that might be appropriate (solution).

HOOK
Imagine that one day you were in a convenience store with your best friend. You saw him/her put candy in his/her pocket and walk out of the store. You wondered if you should tell him to put it back, tell the store clerk, or tell your parents so they could tell his parents about it.
This situation is called a dilemma because you want to keep your friend but you know his action was wrong. It's not a good feeling and you wish you had never seen his action. (Allow some discussion of this scene.) Dilemmas arise in archeology, too. With your group you will read a scenario that happened and you will be asked to recommend action.

EXPLORE
Each year many archeological sites are disturbed and when that happens we lose valuable information about the people who lived there. When artifacts are taken or sites looted, we cannot put the puzzle back together.
Divide the class into six groups and give each group a scenario card. Students will create a short skit based on the scenario described (problem) and include possible action (solution).
Have groups present their skits and discuss as time permits.

REFLECT
Students complete the sentence: "If I found an arrowhead in a state park, I would. . . ."

EVALUATE
Each student will create a poster (8 ½" x 11") or flyer relating the need to protect archeological and historical sites.

SCENARIO CARDS DESCRIBING DILEMMAS

1. You walk by a new house construction project where a crew has been digging a trench for a sewer. You overhear the foremen tell the men to finish the trench and cover up a skeleton that had been disturbed. What would you do?	2. You and some friends are walking home from school. You notice a new ditch opened along the city street and see pottery and bones sticking out. One of your friends pulls out a bone. What would you do?
3. You and your dad go to a gun show at the fairgrounds. In one booth you see some cannon balls that look interesting. The salesman tells you that he got them in the bay when he was dragging a net for shrimp. What would you do?	4. You are fishing with your aunt in the lake along a federal nature preserve. You see several people with shovels and a screen, digging into a bank and removing large pots. What would you do?
5. You go to a garage sale in your neighborhood with your mom. On one table is a collection of arrowheads for sale for $1 each. The owner says he collected them on a hunting lease, where the owner told him he could take them. What would you do?	6. You and a friend are riding your bikes along a country road. You notice that construction for a new state highway has exposed a group of old, antique bottles. No one is around because it is the weekend. What would you do?

Lesson J: Careers: Find Opportunities

OVERVIEW

Lesson Summary: Students will learn about volunteer and career opportunities in archeology.

GETTING STARTED

Levels: grades 4–8

Subjects: technology, social studies, science, language arts, visual arts

Skills: critical thinking skills to organize and use information acquired from a variety of sources including electronic technology; communication skills for written and visual forms; problem-solving and decision-making skills; working independently.

Time: 45–60 minute class period

Class size: any

RESOURCES

Books

Archeology: Boy Scouts of America merit badge booklet

Internet Connections — Using Technology

www.saa.org Society for American Archeology. Information on careers and colleges that offer archeology around the country.

www.About.com Browse by topic. Current news, articles, books and careers.

www.archaeologychannel.org Sites with streaming video and current articles. Also has teacher resources.

www.nps.gov National Park Service. Features "Links to the Past" about archeology in national parks.

www.americanhistory.si.edu/hohr/ springer Smithsonian Museum. Historical archeology and learning from primary sources.

www.ArchaeoVolunteers.org Worldwide network for volunteers.

www.archaeology.com Archaeological Institute of America. Offers a bulletin on field opportunities each summer season.

www.thc.state.tx.us The Texas Historical Commission, preservation agency for Texas.

www.txarch.org Texas Archeological Society. Shows opportunities for networking as volunteer. Segment on careers.

MATERIALS AND EQUIPMENT NEEDED

Access to Internet for most recent information.

CONTENT BRIEF

Students are often interested in archeology but may not know where to learn about it. There are local avocational societies that invite participants to learn field and lab procedures. There are also many universities that offer degrees preparing for careers in archeology.

This lesson will encourage students to discover more about the profession and to join a local group to see if they like the work. Also, take this opportunity to clarify differences between paleontologists and archeologists.

LESSON STRUCTURE:
W.H.E.R.E.

Where is this lesson going; **H**ook students with interesting information. **E**xplore the details of the history and enable the student to learn. **R**eflect on new learning. **E**valuate student learning during the lesson

WHERE
Students will learn about (1) volunteer and (2) career opportunities in the field of archeology.

HOOK
Say: Have you ever wondered how Indiana Jones or Lara Croft got to be archeologists?

EXPLORE
Using the Internet, consult several sites to learn about volunteer or career opportunities in archeology.

REFLECT
What is important to you as you consider career choices: salary, location, service, intellectual challenge? Make a grid or chart that shows these ideas. Evaluate archeology as a career.

EVALUATE
Have students write letters to archeologists asking to volunteer on a project.
Suggested paragraphs for the letter:
1. introduction of self
2. desire to learn for experience
3. interest in archeology
4. previous experience that might contribute to success
5. availability: when you could work, how far will you travel
OR have students write an advertisement as if they were archeologists recruiting volunteers.

Quiz Two

La Salle in Texas,

UNIT TWO:

BE AN

ARCHEOLOGIST

STUDENT NAME _____ DATE _____

1. Archeologists study about

      A. dinosaurs and their environment.
      B. how people lived in the past.
      C. what strata volcanoes laid down.
      D. how rainforests function.

Use the information in the diagram below and your knowledge of social studies to answer question 2.

identify shipwreck >> build a cofferdam >> excavate and screen soil >> map patterns >> analyze artifacts >> write report

2. The best title for the diagram above is

      A. Writing a Report
      B. Mapping Artifacts
      C. Finding Souvenirs
      D. Archeological Process

3. What task is NOT part of an archeologist's job?

      A. Carefully record and map all features and artifacts.
      B. Clean and preserve artifacts for future reference.
      C. Shovel dirt quickly in order to find buried treasure.
      D. Protect important archeological sites from being disturbed.

4. A magnetometer survey can show archeologists . . .

      A. a picture of a shipwreck underwater.
      B. an anomaly or irregularity composed of metal.
      C. wooden ships that sank.
      D. fish that live on a shipwreck.

5. A grid, framework of parallel and crossed lines, is used by archeologists to . . .

      A. map features and artifacts.
      B. set out tents to live in.
      C. direct traffic around a site.
      D. put plants in a garden.

Use the information in the box below and your knowledge of social studies to answer question 6.

> Archeologists identified the following artifacts among
> the cargo on La Belle:
> Wooden crucifix
> Wooden comb
> Ceramic pipe
> Game pieces
> Brass signet

6. Under what category would they be classified?

    A. Trade goods for native Americans
    B. Items for defense against enemies
    C. Objects to set up a house for living
    D. Artifacts used by the crew of *La Belle* personally

7. Fire pots found on *La Belle* would most likely be used by the crew to . . .

    A. cook food.
    B. light their cabins.
    C. set an enemy ship on fire.
    D. warm a tea pot.

8. Hawk bells were used in Europe to . . .

    A. create music.
    B. decorate houses.
    C. call people for dinner.
    D. locate falcons during a hunt.

Use the illustration and your knowledge of social studies to answer question 9:

9. This metal artifact (a needle) would be classified in the following category:

    A. tools
    B. weapons
    C. trade goods
    D. religious items

Use the list and your knowledge of social studies to answer question 10:

Navigation during the 1600s was difficult because . . .
A. No clock could keep time on the oceans.
B. Satellites were controlled by China.
C. Maps were not very accurate.
D. Few mapmakers had seen the coast of Texas.

10. Which statement above does NOT belong in this list?

    A.
    B.
    C.
    D.

Overview

Unit Summary: Students will create mural/maps that show the travels of La Salle in the New World.

ENDURING UNDERSTANDINGS

Exploration of unknown regions is a universal human endeavor.
Human migration expands trade and establishes colonies.

ESSENTIAL QUESTIONS

Why do people risk their lives to explore unknown regions?
Why did the French go to the Gulf of Mexico/Mississippi River?
Where would you like to explore?
How would you feel about leaving home and everything familiar to go to an unknown region?
What was the impact of European exploration on the continent of North America?
What was the Spanish reaction to the French incursion into the Gulf of Mexico?
How has migration affected you?
What French and Spanish influences are noticeable today (phrases, place names, food, music)?

SOCIAL STUDIES STRANDS — NATIONAL COUNCIL FOR SOCIAL STUDIES

Culture (French, colonial)
People, Place, and Environments (journeys in the New World)
Production, Distribution, and Consumption (colonial system, trade)
Global Connections (colonial system, European politics)

CURRICULUM STANDARDS FOR SOCIAL STUDIES — NATIONAL COUNCIL FOR SOCIAL STUDIES

Identify and describe historic periods and patterns of change, such as the growth of the colonial system.
Elaborate mental maps of locales, regions, and the world that demonstrate understanding of relative location, directions, size, and shape.
Create, interpret, and use various representations of the earth.
Locate and describe varying landforms and geographic features.
Explain why things are located where they are.
Use appropriate resources, data sources, and geographic tools to

generate, manipulate, and interpret information.

Use economic concepts to help explain historical developments.

Explain how goods and services are distributed.

Describe and analyze the effects of changing technologies.

Work independently and cooperatively to accomplish goals.

TEKS:

4.2, 4.3, 4.6, 4.8, 4.9, 4.10, 4.11, 4.20, 4.22, 4.23, 4.24

5.1, 5.6, 5.9, 5.10, 5.11, 5.25, 5.26, 5.27

6.2, 6.3, 6.7, 6.8, 6.14, 6.15, 6.16, 6.21, 6.22, 6.23

7.1, 7.2, 7.11, 7.16, 7.23, 7.25, 7.26

8.1, 8.2, 8.10, 8.11, 8.20, 8.24, 8.30, 8.31, 8.32

EXTEND ACROSS THE CURRICULUM

See page 115 for lesson ideas that will extend the study of La Salle into many subject areas.

Getting Started

Level: grades 4–8

Subjects: social studies, history, geography, language arts, math, technology, visual arts

Skills: critical-thinking skills to organize and use information acquired from a variety of sources including electronic technology; communication skills for written, oral and visual forms; problem-solving and decision-making skills; skills to work independently and with others in a variety of settings.

Time: 5 class periods approximately 45–60 minutes each

Class size: 24–32 students divided into four groups for study, mural production, and presentation

RESOURCES FOR UNIT *principal resources for this unit in **bold**.

Books

*Bruseth, James E. and Toni Turner. *From a Watery Grave: The Discovery and Excavation of La Salle's Shipwreck, La Belle.* College Station: Texas A&M University Press, 2005 (referred to as *FWG*).** Adult to intermediate level. A detailed account of the recovery of *La Belle*. Many photographs and illustrations. Some primary accounts are quoted. Excellent bibliography.

Audiovisuals

Dreams of Conquest (DVD). **Alan Govenar, Documentary Arts, 2004.** *Please observe content advisory for this DVD, p. 112.*

Internet Connections — Using Technology

www.tsha.utexas.edu/handbook/online Handbook of Texas Online. Presents short articles related to *La Belle* and La Salle.

http://www.civilization.ca/vmnf/vmnfe.asp Virtual Museum of New France. Highlights the French in the New World.

www.thc.state.tx.us/lasalle Texas Historical Commission, state agency for preservation. Provides articles and timelines for life and times of La Salle.

www.libraries.uta.edu/ccon/ Cartographic Connections: Improving Teaching through the Use of Historic Maps.

www.americanjourneys.org/aj-124b Eyewitness Accounts of Early American Exploration and Settlement, University of Wisconsin. Primary documents and maps.

www.enchantedlearning.com/explorers Good information on La Salle and maps on the travels.

MATERIALS AND EQUIPMENT NEEDED

4 road maps of your state for student use

4 atlases or world maps for student reference

Example of early maps of North America — Ex: 1692 Rouillard from Le Clerieq (http://www.library.upenn.edu/exhibits/rbm/kislak/lands/nfmap.html or others from the Internet).

Projector for DVD

DVD *Dreams of Conquest*

Bruseth, *From A Watery Grave*

Internet for technology connection

Outline map (North America) to make transparency for creating murals; optional copy for each student

Transparency of early map

4 large sheets of paper (48" x 36") for murals

6 smaller sheets of paper per group (4" by 5½") for illustrations

4 sets of markers

Space for display of murals, tape/tacks to mount murals

Copy of INSTRUCTIONS for each GROUP (4 groups)

Copies of key pages from *FWG* for GROUPS to use (3 copies p. 9; 1 copy p. 25)

Copies of CHART ABOUT LA SAL-
LE'S JOURNEYS, one for each
student
Copies of SHORT ANSWERS, one
for each student

Content Brief

The French explorer, Robert Cavelier, Sieur de la Salle, made several
important discoveries and claims in
North America. He traveled to Canada (New France) in 1666 to join his
brother, Abbé Cavelier. The French
had a strong hold on the St. Lawrence River and Great Lakes, where
they made alliances with the Native Americans. La Salle established
several outposts in the Great Lakes
region and learned from the Native
Americans about a river that led to
the sea. Many explorers wanted to
find a route to China across North
America, so La Salle hoped the river
would lead to the Pacific Ocean. He
made several trips of exploration,
then on one trip he connected with
the Mississippi River and paddled
south to the Gulf of Mexico. He
claimed all territory drained by the
Mississippi River for France and
named it Louisiana in honor of King
Louis XIV. After this trip La Salle
had a new focus.

La Salle decided that he wanted
to build a large trading post at the
mouth of the Mississippi River
where he could get a lot of busi-
ness from European nations as they
settled the New World. He went to
Paris to get approval from King Louis XIV for this plan. Since Louis XIV
was at war with Spain at the time, he
gave La Salle permission to settle a
colony that would be in Spanish territory. He also gave La Salle funds to
finance the expedition.

La Salle gathered supplies and
sailed from France, crossing the Atlantic Ocean. On the voyage, Spanish pirates captured one of his four
ships. After making some repairs
and getting supplies in the West Indies, La Salle started into the Gulf of
Mexico, controlled by the Spanish.
The expedition sighted land just
west of the Mississippi River but did
not recognize the area.

They continued west along the
coast and decided to explore Matagorda Bay. While *La Belle* sailed
into the bay easily, the supply ship,
L'Aimable, wrecked in Pass Cavallo.
The expedition camped on Matagorda Island while they looked for a
better location to build a settlement.
The military escort, *Le Joly*, sailed
back to France with some colonists
who did not want to stay. Fort St.
Louis was built on Garcitas Creek,
which flowed into Matagorda Bay.
La Salle continued to search for the
Mississippi River. While La Salle
and some men were in East Texas, a
storm raged in Matagorda Bay and
sank *La Belle* beyond repair. It was
their last ship, their only remaining
vessel for exploration and transport.

La Salle secured Fort St. Louis and
left some colonists there. He knew
that he had to make contact with the
French settlements in Canada. He
led a small band of men toward the
Mississippi River, but was killed by
members of the party in East Texas.
Several other murders and deser-
tions resulted, but Joutel led a few
men on to the French outpost on
the Arkansas River. They completed
a trek of about 1200 miles back to
Canada and, eventually, returned to
France.

The colonists who remained at
Fort St. Louis on Garcitas Creek
were weakened by lack of supplies
and disease. In January 1689, a year
after La Salle left, the Karankawa
killed most of the colonists. Some
Karankawa women protected several
French children, who were later rescued by the Spanish and eventually
returned to France. A few months
after the massacre, a Spanish expedition found the fort and buried the
French cannons and bodies they
found.

While La Salle did not succeed in
establishing a colony on the Mississippi River, he did establish French
claims to territory drained by the
Mississippi River. The French returned to the Gulf of Mexico and established Mobile, Alabama and New
Orleans, Louisiana by 1699. Several
members of La Salle's expedition
traveled with those settlers. La Salle
is remembered as a great explorer
and many places and institutions are
named for him.

The Spanish considered the
French to be intruders into their
territory. As a result of La Salle's
expedition, they concentrated on
building more settlements in Texas
in the early 1700s. The Spanish even
returned to the site of Fort St. Louis
and built Presidio Nuestra Senora
de Loreto y La Bahia directly on
top of the ruins of Fort St. Louis.
Across Garcitas Creek, they built
the first of several missions, known
as Espiritu Santo. The last of those
missions is preserved in a state park
today at Goliad, Texas. The Spanish

influence in Texas and the Southwest continues today through the descendants of those Spanish who came to thwart the French threat to their territory.

La Salle's attempt to set up a colony on the shores of the Gulf of Mexico caused the Spanish to renew their colonial efforts in Texas and had a lasting impact on Texas history and culture.

VOCABULARY

Word bank for notebook or word wall for easy reference. Additional vocabulary is defined in the glossary.

Buccaneers: French pirates on the Caribbean islands who were named from the smoked meat they prepared (from French word "boucaner" [pronounced boo-kan-AY], to smoke or dry meat)

Karankawa: Native Americans along the Gulf coast

Mission: an organization sent for the spread of religion; also the buildings for that purpose

Outpost: settlement on the edge of frontier, often had trade goods and sometimes served as a fort

Presidio: the fort, often near a mission, to protect a settlement

UNIT STRUCTURE: W.H.E.R.E.

Where is this lesson going; **H**ook students with interesting information; **E**xplore the details and enable the students to learn; **R**eflect on new learning; **E**valuate and assess student learning during the lesson.

WHERE

Student groups will prepare a mural/map of one of La Salle's journeys with picture inserts about various encounters along the way. Group assignments are (1) France to Canada, (2) France to Caribbean Sea, (3) Gulf of Mexico, and (4) Texas to Canada.

Students will individually complete a CHART ABOUT LA SALLE'S JOURNEYS. Optional: individual maps of journeys.

Students will discuss and write short answers to the questions posed in Facets of Understanding.

HOOK

Class 1: Brainstorm student experience with maps.

Ask students: Have you used a map? What did it show you? How was it useful?

Provide several state road maps for class use. Have a student record group answers to the following questions on the board: Where are you? How would you get from your town to the state capital? What is the distance? What direction would you be going? How long would it take you, traveling at 55 miles per hour?

Ask students: In the late 1600s, what maps did LaSalle have to use? (Show transparency of Rouillard 1692 or another early map.) How accurate or helpful were they?

EXPLORE

Class 1: Divide the students into four groups. Each group will create a mural/map of one of La Salle's journeys. Assign a journey to each group: (1) France to Canada, (2) France to Caribbean Sea, (3) Gulf of Mexico, (4) Texas to Canada. INSTRUCTIONS sheets for each group will detail their tasks.

Show the DVD *Dreams of Conquest* to give students an overview of La Salle's journeys (PLEASE NOTE CONTENT WARNING IN GUIDE TO *DREAMS OF CONQUEST*, p. 112). See Guide to *Dreams of Conquest* for more details. See SYNOPSIS of the DVD in Guide to choose short chapters if time is limited.

OR give overview by making transparencies of *FWG* pages 9, 21, & 25 and briefly introduce the unit by reading the BACKGROUND information (p. 61–62).

Class 2: Provide INSTRUCTIONS, mural size sheet of paper (48" x 36"), six sheets of paper (4" x 5½"), and markers to each GROUP. Tasks are defined on the INSTRUCTIONS sheet for each group. Make available texts, DVD and Internet connections and sites to use for research.

Ask students to research incidents, draw illustration, and note dates as well as locations on the maps.

Class 3: Students continue research and work on mural/maps.

Class 4: Each GROUP will present their mural/map to the class with comments on the illustrations. Students will take notes on CHART ABOUT LA SALLE'S JOURNEYS (student worksheet) as presentations are given.

Class 5: Continue presentations. Students complete CHART ABOUT LA SALLE'S JOURNEYS and discuss or write SHORT ANSWERS (student worksheet) to the questions posed in Facets of Understanding. Collect and score student work.

REFLECT

Ask students: How are French and Spanish influences still noticeable today (phrases, place names, food, music, language)? Have students give multiple answers.

EVALUATE

Rubrics found in the STANDARDS section of PERFORMANCE TASKS.

(Group) Each group will present information from their mural/map to the class.

(Individual) Each student will prepare CHART ABOUT LA SALLE'S JOURNEYS from presentations of the groups. Optional: Students will mark journeys on individual maps. Each student participates in discussion by answering the questions from Facets of Understanding (or completes SHORT ANSWERS worksheet for

the questions posed in Facets of Understanding).

FACETS OF UNDERSTANDING INTEGRATED INTO THE UNIT

Interpretation: Why do people risk their lives to explore unknown regions?

Self-knowledge: Where would you like to explore?

Empathy: How would you feel about leaving home and everything familiar to go to an unknown region?

Explanation: What was the impact of European exploration on the continent of North America?

Perspective: What was the Spanish reaction to the French incursion into the Gulf of Mexico?

Application: How are French and Spanish influences still noticeable today (phrases, place names, food, music, language)?

Student Pages

La Salle in Texas,
UNIT THREE:
JOURNEYS
IN THE NEW
WORLD

INSTRUCTIONS FOR GROUP ONE

Your group will create a mural/map that will show one journey that La Salle made in the New World. You will divide the tasks among your group (see suggested tasks for group members).

Tasks for students

a) Using the chart TRAVELS FROM FRANCE TO CANADA and questions below as a start, research the incidents listed. Complete the section in the chart labeled OUTCOME.

b) Each student will illustrate, label, and date one incident that happened along the way (see chart below for incidents and also REFERENCE for more information).

c) 2 students will trace map onto mural paper.

d) 2 students will label geographic features on mural.

e) 2 students will attach the illustrations to the mural.

f) One student will present information about the journey on your mural to the class.

g) All students will take notes on a CHART ABOUT LA SALLE'S JOURNEYS as the four journeys are presented, then write SHORT ANSWERS to questions. (Your teacher may make individual map assignments.)

Questions to consider before you begin the mural:

Why do people risk their lives to explore unknown regions?

How would you feel about leaving home and everything familiar to go to an unknown region?

What was the impact of European exploration on the continent of North America?

How has migration affected you?

What French and Spanish influences are noticeable today (phrases, place names, food, music)?

Why was Canada called "New France"?

Why was the territory claimed by La Salle called "Louisiana"?

Materials

Copy of *FWG* page 9 for easy reference

Atlas or world map for reference

Set of color markers to create mural

Mural size paper for group mural (48" x 36")

Paper for individual student illustrations of incidents (4" x 5 1/2")

LOCATION	DATE	INCIDENT	OUTCOME	REFERENCE
(1) La Rochelle, France to Quebec, Canada	1666	La Salle left Jesuit order and traveled to New World		www.civilization.ca/vmnf
Montreal, Canada	1666–1670	La Salle joined his brother, Abbé Cavelier		*FWG* p. 16
Kingston on Lake Ontario	1673	Built Fort Frontenac as outpost		www.civilization.ca/vmnf
Mackinac (Mich.)	1679 Aug.	La Salle sailed across the Great Lakes with *Griffon* (ship)		www.civilization.ca/vmnf
Fort Prud'homme near Memphis, Tenn.	1682 Feb.	Established trading post for Shawnee, Illinois, & Miami tribes		*FWG* p. 20
Mississippi River (Venice, La.) then back to Quebec, Canada	1682 April	La Salle traveled down Mississippi River to the mouth and claimed land for France		*FWG* pp. 16–17

Student Pages

La Salle in Texas,

UNIT THREE:

JOURNEYS

IN THE NEW

WORLD

Group Two — France to Caribbean Sea

INSTRUCTIONS FOR GROUP TWO

Your group will create a mural/map that will show one journey that La Salle made in the New World. You will divide the tasks among your group (see suggested tasks for group members).

Tasks for students

a) Using the chart TRAVELS FROM FRANCE TO CARIBBEAN SEA and questions below as a start, research the incidents listed. Complete the section labeled OUTCOME.

b) Each student will illustrate, label, and date one incident that happened along the way (see chart below for incidents and also REFERENCE for more information).

c) 2 students will trace map onto mural paper.

d) 2 students will label geographic features on mural.

e) 2 students will attach the illustrations to the mural.

f) One student will present the journey on your mural to the class.

g) All students will take notes on a CHART ABOUT LA SALLE'S JOURNEYS as the four journeys are presented, then write SHORT ANSWERS to questions. (Your teacher may make individual map assignments.)

Questions to consider before you begin the mural:

Why do people risk their lives to explore unknown regions?

How did La Salle recruit people to sail with him?

What was the impact of European exploration on the continent of North America?

Why are the Caribbean islands called "West Indies"?

Why did some members of the expedition stay in the West Indies?

What is the origin of the term "buccaneers"?

What was the Spanish reaction to the French incursion into the Gulf of Mexico?

How has migration affected you?

What French and Spanish influences are noticeable today (phrases, place names, food, music)?

Materials

Copy of page 9 *FWG* for easy reference

Set of color markers to draw mural

Mural size paper for group (36" x 48")

Paper for individual student illustrations (4" x 5½")

LOCATION	DATE	INCIDENT	OUTCOME	REFERENCE
Paris, France	1683	La Salle (LS) asked Louis XIV for money to outfit the expedition		*FWG* pp. 19–20, 22
Rochefort, France	1684	LS got supplies and ships for voyage from the depot		*FWG* pp. 24, 66, 68, 105
La Rochelle, France	1684 Aug.	Sailed with 4 ships: *L'Aimable, Le Joly, Le Saint Francois, La Belle*		*FWG* pp. 24
Hispanola/Santa Domingo (West Indies)	1684 Sept.	*Le Saint Francois* captured by Spanish pirates		*FWG* pp. 21
Petit Groave, Haiti (West Indies)	1684 Oct.– Nov.	Gathered supplies; Sailor, Denis Thomas and six others, stayed in Haiti with buccaneers		*FWG* pp . 7, 9, 11
Louisiana Coast, Mississippi River (Venice, La.)	1685 Jan.	Sighted land — didn't recognize Mississippi River		*FWG* pp. 12, 21

La Salle in Texas,

UNIT THREE:
JOURNEYS
IN THE NEW
WORLD

INSTRUCTIONS FOR GROUP THREE

Your group will create a mural/map that will show one journey that La Salle made in the New World. You will divide the tasks among your group (see suggested tasks for group members).

Tasks for students

a) Using the chart TRAVELS ALONG THE GULF COAST and questions below as a start, research the incidents listed. Complete the section labeled OUTCOME.

b) Each student will illustrate, label and date one incident that happened along the way (see chart below for incidents and also REFERENCE for more information).

c) 2 students will trace map onto mural paper.

d) 2 students will label geographic features on mural.

e) 2 students will attach the illustrations to the mural.

f) One student will present the journey on your mural to the class.

g) All students will take notes on a CHART ABOUT LA SALLE'S JOURNEYS as the four journeys are presented then write SHORT ANSWERS to questions. (Your teacher may make individual map assignments.)

Questions to consider before you begin the mural:

Why do people risk their lives to explore unknown regions?

Why did the French go to the Gulf of Mexico/Mississippi River?

Why didn't La Salle recognize the mouth of the Mississippi River?

How would you feel about leaving home and everything familiar to go to an unknown region?

What was the impact of European exploration on the continent of North America?

Why did La Salle travel up Garcitas Creek to build the fort?

How has migration affected you?

What French and Spanish influences are still noticeable today (phrases, place names, food, music)?

Materials

Copy of page 25 *FWG* for easy reference

Atlas or world map for reference

Set of color markers to draw mural

Mural size paper for group (36" x 48")

Paper for individual student illustration (4" x 5½")

GROUP THREE: TRAVELS ALONG THE GULF OF MEXICO

LOCATION	DATE	INCIDENT	OUTCOME	REFERENCE
(3) Matagorda Island near Cedar Bayou, Tx.	1685 Feb.	Crew put ashore to find mouth of river		*FWG* p. 26
Matagorda Bay through Pass Cavallo	1685 Feb.	*La Belle* entered bay, *L'Aimable* wrecked in pass		*FWG* pp. 25–26
Grand Camp, Matagorda Island	1685 Mar.	Set up to hold supplies and colonists, *Le Joly* returned to France		*FWG* p. 25
Fort St. Louis, Garcitas Creek, Texas	1685–1689	Built fort on high bluff — 180 colonists		*FWG* pp. 8, 27
Fort St. Louis to Nacogdoches, return	1686 Jan. depart; May return	La Salle with 20 men leaves *La Belle* to go east to look for Mississippi River		www.thc.state.tx.us/lasalle
Matagorda Bay	1686 Jan.	*La Belle* wrecked in storm; survivors return to Fort St. Louis in May		www.thc.state.tx.us/lasalle

La Salle in Texas,

UNIT THREE:
JOURNEYS
IN THE NEW
WORLD

INSTRUCTIONS FOR GROUP FOUR

Your group will create a mural/map that will show one journey that La Salle made in the New World. You will divide the tasks among your group (see suggested tasks for group members).

Tasks for students

a) Using the chart TRAVELS ACROSS TEXAS TO CANADA and questions below as a start, research the incidents listed. Complete the section labeled OUTCOME.

b) Each student will illustrate, label, and date one incident that happened along the way (see chart below for incidents and also REFERENCE for more information).

c) 2 students will trace map onto mural paper.

d) 2 students will label geographic features on mural.

e) 2 students will attach the illustrations to the mural.

f) One student will present a summary of the journey on your mural to the class.

g) All students will take notes on a CHART ABOUT LA SALLE'S JOURNEYS as four journeys are presented then write SHORT ANSWERS to questions. (Your teacher may make individual map assignments.)

Questions to discuss before you begin the mural.

Why do people risk their lives to explore unknown regions?

Why did the French go to the Gulf of Mexico/Mississippi River?

Why did La Salle set out on foot for Canada?

Why did La Salle's men murder him?

What was the impact of European exploration on the continent of North America?

What was the Spanish reaction to the French incursion into the Gulf of Mexico?

How has migration affected you?

What French and Spanish influences are still noticeable today (phrases, place names, food, music)?

Materials

Copy of page 9 *FWG* for easy reference

Atlas or world map for reference

Set of color markers to create mural

Large mural paper for group (36" x 48")

Paper for individual student illustrations (4" x 5 ½")

LOCATION	DATE	INCIDENT	OUTCOME	REFERENCE
Fort St. Louis, Garcitas Creek, Texas	1687 Jan. 12	La Salle and 16 men set out for Canada		*FWG* pp. 8, 27
Navasota, Texas	1687 Mar.	La Salle ambushed and killed by part of group		*FWG* pp. 30–31
Arkansas River outpost	1687	Small group of men (7) continue toward Canada; others stay in Texas and New Mexico		*FWG* p. 29
Fort St. Louis on the Illinois River at Starved Rock, Ill.	1688	Men reach settlements in New France		*FWG* p. 29
Montreal (July) then Quebec (Aug.)	1688	Men complete journey of 1200 miles		*FWG* p. 29
La Rochelle, France	1688 Oct.	Seven men including Joutel returned to France to tell their story		*FWG* p. 29
ADDENDUM (Garcitas Creek, Texas)	1689 Jan.	Indians attack Fort St. Louis, killing all but five children; Spanish arrive at fort in April		*FWG* p. 28

La Salle in Texas,

UNIT THREE: JOURNEYS IN THE NEW WORLD

PERFORMANCE TASKS — G.R.A.S.P.S.

The acronym G.R.A.S.P.S. stand for **G**oal, **R**ole, **A**udience, **S**ituation, **P**roduct, **S**tandards.

Goal

The goal is to illustrate the extent and importance of La Salle's journeys in the New World by creating four murals/maps. Also note the resulting French and Spanish influences in North America today.

Role

You are responsible for contributing to the mural/map, completing your CHART ABOUT LA SALLE'S JOURNEYS (optional individual maps) and writing SHORT ANSWERS to the questions from Facets of Understanding.

Audience

Your class will learn from your presentation.

Situation

To understand the extent of La Salle's journeys in the 1600s, you will create a mural showing his routes.

Products

(*Group*) Mural/map of La Salle's journeys

(*Individual*) CHART ABOUT LA SALLE'S JOURNEYS (optional individual map)

(*Individual*) Discussion or SHORT ANSWERS worksheet for questions from Facets of Understanding

Standards — Assessment

RUBRICS for evaluation

Students may create criteria for evaluation or use the following.

(*Group*) mural/map of journeys

Level 4 (highest): Map/mural shows route with 6 incidents illustrated, labeled and dated. The map/mural is clear, colorful, neat, and accurate. It has the following 10 components: title, authors, due date for project, compass rose, scale, oceans, continents, countries, cities, title on each illustration.

Level 3: Map/mural shows route and 6 incidents. Only 7–8 components are on the map. The map is modestly clear, colorful, neat, or accurate.

Level 2: Map/mural shows route and only 4 incidents. Only 4–6 components are on the map. The map is not clear, colorful, neat, or accurate.

Level 1: Map/mural shows route and only 2 incidents. Only 1–3 components are on the map. The map is incomplete, messy, and missing important information.

Student Pages

La Salle in Texas,

UNIT THREE:

JOURNEYS

IN THE NEW

WORLD

(Individual) CHART ABOUT LA SALLE'S JOURNEYS

Level 4 (highest): The chart is complete with information on 4 journeys and outcomes. Outcomes show significance of location and incident in historical context. Short answer is well-defined.

Level 3: The chart shows information on 3 journeys and outcomes. Outcomes show thought about location and incident in historical context. Short answer is OK.

Level 2: The chart shows information on 2 journeys and outcomes. Outcomes are listed with minimum information. Short answer is minimal.

Level 1: The chart shows information on 1 or no journeys. Outcomes are incomplete. Short answer is incomplete.

SHORT ANSWERS for Facets of Understanding (individual)

Level 4 (highest): Essay assignment is complete and detailed in answers, shows analysis and interpretation in historical context. Six (6) questions from Facets of Understanding are complete. Essays are well-developed with main points supported by facts. Writing is grammatical with correct spelling. Essays are neat and easy to read.

Level 3: Essay assignment is detailed in answers, shows thought. Four (4) questions from Facets of Understanding are complete. Essays are clear with few grammatical and spelling errors. Essays are neat and easy to read.

Level 2: Essay shows thought. Two (2) questions from Facets of Understanding are answered. Essays are clear with some grammatical and spelling errors. Essays are neat and easy to read.

Level 1: Essay is incomplete and lacks detail in answers, shows some analysis and interpretation in historical context. One (1) or none of the questions from Facets of Understanding are answered. Essays are unclear, with grammatical and spelling errors. Essays are incomplete and messy.

Optional INDIVIDUAL MAPS by students.

Level 4 (highest): Map shows 4 routes labeled and dated. The map is clear, neat, and accurate. It has the following 10 components: title, authors, due date for project, compass rose, scale, oceans, continents, countries, cities, title on each illustration.

Level 3: Map shows 3 routes, labeled and dated. Only 7–8 components are on the map. The map is modestly clear, neat, or accurate.

Level 2: Map shows 2 routes, labeled and dated. Only 4–6 components are on the map. The map is not clear, neat, or accurate.

Level 1: Map shows 1 or no routes. Only 1–3 components are on the map. The map is incomplete, messy, and missing important information.

Name _____ Date _____

Chart about La Salle's Journeys

Take notes as presentations are made. Use your notes to discuss
and write SHORT ANSWERS to questions from Facets of Understanding.

LOCATION	DATES	OUTCOME
(1) France to Canada (and the Mississippi River)		
(2) France to Caribbean Sea		
(3) Along Gulf of Mexico		
(4) Texas to Canada (and France)		

Name _____ Date _____

Student Pages

La Salle in Texas,

UNIT THREE:

JOURNEYS

IN THE NEW

WORLD

Short Answers for Facets of Understanding

Answer the following questions with complete sentences.

1. *Interpretation:* Why do people risk their lives to explore unknown regions?

2. *Self-knowledge:* Where would you like to explore?

3. *Empathy:* How would you feel about leaving home and everything familiar to go to an unknown region?

4. *Explanation:* What was the impact of European exploration on the continent of North America?

5. *Perspective:* What was the Spanish reaction to the French incursion into the Gulf of Mexico?

6. *Application:* How are French and Spanish influences noticeable today (phrases, place names, food, music, language)?

KEY to DATA// LOCATION	DATE	INCIDENT	OUTCOME	SOURCE
(1) La Rochelle, France to Quebec, Canada	1666	La Salle (LS) left Jesuit order and traveled to New World	French stronghold in Canada had settlements	www .civilization .ca/vmnf
Montreal, Canada	1666–1670	La Salle joined his brother, Abbe Cavelier to explore and set up posts	La Salle traded and learned Indian languages	*FWG* p. 16
Kingston on Lake Ontario	1673	After several successful trading posts, LS Built Fort Frontenac as outpost	La Salle helped the French expand claims	www .civilization .ca/vmnf
Mackinac (Mich.)	1679	La Salle sailed the *Griffon* (ship) across the Great Lakes	The *Griffon* sank on voyage back to Montreal	www .civilization .ca/vmnf
Fort Prud'homme near Memphis, Tenn.	1682 (Feb.)	Established trading post for Shawnee, Illinois & Miami tribes	LS reached farther into present day United States	*FWG* p. 20
Mississippi R (Venice, La.) Then back to Quebec, Canada	1682 (April)	LS traveled down Mississippi River to the mouth and claimed land for French King Louis XIV, hence Louisiana	France claimed about ⅓ of the North American continent	*FWG* pp. 16–17
(2) Paris, France	1683	To obtain permission and funding from Louis XIV to set up a trading post	Louis XIV wanted to challenge Spain	*FWG* pp. 19–20, 22
Rochefort, France	1684	Depot to get supplies and ships for voyage	Depot set up to supply goods for exploration	*FWG* pp. 24, 66, 68, 105
La Rochelle, France	1684 (Aug.)	Sailed with 4 ships: *L'Aimable, Le Joly, Le Saint Francois, La Belle*	300 people wanted to go to the New World	*FWG* p. 24
Hispanola/Santa Domingo (West Indies)	1684 (Sept.)	*Le Saint Francois* captured by Spanish pirates	Spanish were alerted to LS mission	*FWG* p. 21
Petit Groave, Haiti (West Indies)	1684 Oct.– Nov.	Gathered supplies; Sailor, Denis Thomas and six others, stayed in Haiti with buccaneers	Some colonists were afraid to go into Gulf	*FWG* pp. 7, 9, 11
Louisiana Coast, Mississippi River (Venice, La.)	1685 (Jan.)	Sighted land — didn't recognize Mississippi River	Did not get established	*FWG* pp. 12, 21

KEY to DATA// LOCATION	DATE	INCIDENT	OUTCOME	SOURCE
(3) Matagorda Island near Cedar Bayou, Tx.	1685 (Feb.)	Crew put ashore to find mouth of river	Disappointed at not finding large river	*FWG* p. 26
Matagorda Bay through Pass Cavallo	1685 (Feb.)	*La Belle* entered bay, *L'Aimable* wrecked in pass	Many supplies were lost	*FWG* pp. 25–26
Grand Camp, Matagorda Island	1685 (Mar.)	Set up to hold supplies and colonists, *Le Joly* returned to France	Short term solution	*FWG* p. 25
Fort St. Louis, Garcitas Creek	1685–1689	Fort built by French — 180 colonists	Well-protected, away from the bay and Gulf	*FWG* pp. 8, 27
Fort St. Louis to Nacogdoches, return	1686 (Jan.)	La Salle with 50 men leaves *La Belle* to go east to look for Mississippi River	Established trading relations with Caddo	www.thc .state.tx.us/ lasalle
Matagorda Bay	1686 (Jan.)	*La Belle* wrecked in storm; survivors returned to Fort St. Louis in May	They were stranded, no way back to France	www.thc .state.tx.us/ lasalle
(4) Fort St. Louis, Garcitas Creek	1687 (Jan. 12)	La Salle and sixteen men set out for Canada	Set out on unknown route	*FWG* pp. 8, 27
Navasota, Texas	1687 (Mar.)	La Salle ambushed by part of group	Killings weakened group	*FWG* pp. 30–31
Arkansas River outpost	1687	Small group of men (7) continue toward Canada; some stay in Texas	Unsure of route	*FWG* p. 29
Fort St. Louis on the Illinois River	1688	Men reach New France	Knew they could return	*FWG* p. 29
Montreal (July) then Quebec (Aug.)	1688	Men complete journey of 1200 miles	Told story of expedition	*FWG* p. 29
La Rochelle, France	1688 (Oct.)	Six men, including Joutel, returned to France to tell their story	Other expeditions knew more	*FWG* p. 29
ADDENDUM Garcitas Creek, Texas	1689 (Jan.)	Karankawa attack Fort St. Louis, killing all but five children; Spanish arrive in Apr.	Spanish mapped fort and returned in 1722	*FWG* p. 28

Extend across the Curriculum

Math

1) Problems related to voyages:

a) How many days did it take La Salle to cross the Atlantic Ocean? He left France August 1, 1684 and arrived in Haiti/Santo Domingo September 27, 1684.

b) La Salle set sail from Santo Domingo on November 25, 1684 and arrived on the Gulf Coast January 1, 1685. How many days did he sail?

c) How many total days did he sail from France to the Gulf Coast?

d) Use the number of total days La Salle traveled and assume that he traveled 5,000 miles. How far did he travel each day, on average?

e) If La Salle only sailed 10 hours each day, how fast was the expedition traveling?

f) Today a plane averages 625 miles per hour. How many hours would the same 5,000-mile trip take?

g) Calculate the trek from Texas to Canada. The surviving Frenchmen walked from Texas to Canada (approximately 1200 miles) after *La Belle* was wrecked in the storm. Calculate how long it takes for you to walk one (1) mile. If you walked 8 hours a day, how many days would it take you to walk the same distance as the French trek in 1687–88?

Language Arts

1) Create an advertisement to recruit colonists to sail with La Salle.

2) Write a journal entry as a historical character (La Salle, Joutel, Abbé Cavelier, King Louis XIV, Madame Talon, or others) or recall an event or occasion of importance to you and write a journal entry about that.

Science

1) Research and use navigational instruments.

Social Studies

1) You have been selected to set up a colony (in 1600s on the Gulf coast or today on the moon). Create a plan that would include considerations about location, what to do if the land is already inhabited, supplies to pack, what work needs to be done on arrival, and who will go.

2) Enter the National History Day competition using information about La Salle that you learned in this unit. Theme for 2007: Triumph and Tragedy in History; 2008: The Individual in History. See National History Day web site for more details (www.national historyday.org/).

Geography

1) Comparing maps. Find a map of the time of La Salle (1692 by Rouillard or others from the Internet) to see how geographic features were shown in 1600s. Overlay a modern map of North America on one of these to see reasons why La Salle missed the mouth of the Mississippi River when he sailed along the coast in 1684.

2) What different environments did the expedition pass through?

Visual Arts/Geography

1) Create a board game based on La Salle's journeys, or develop as a computer game.

STUDENT NAME _____ DATE _____

Quiz Three

La Salle in Texas,
UNIT THREE:
JOURNEYS
IN THE NEW
WORLD

A Turning Point in History
During this period, Europeans conquered major portions of the world. They set up colonies to gain wealth and convert the native peoples to Christianity. Colonizers established European style governments and economies around the world.

1. The best title for the description of this turning point in history (above) would be

   A. Protestant Reformation (ca. 1500–1650)
   B. The Cold War (1945–1991)
   C. The Classical Period (ca. 1000 B.C.–A.D. 500)
   D. The Age of Exploration and Colonization (ca. 1450–1900)

Use the information in the box below and your knowledge of social studies to answer question 2

The French explorer, Robert Cavelier, Sieur de la Salle, traveled to Canada (New France) in 1666 to join his brother, Abbé Cavelier. The French had a strong hold on the St. Lawrence River and Great Lakes, where they made alliances with the Native Americans. La Salle established several outposts in the Great Lakes region and learned from the Native Americans about a river that led to the sea. Many explorers wanted to find a route to China across North America, so La Salle hoped the river would lead to the Pacific Ocean. He made several trips of exploration, then on one trip he connected with the Mississippi River and paddled south to the Gulf of Mexico. He claimed all territory drained by the Mississippi River for France and named it Louisiana in honor of King Louis XIV.

2. The best title for the above narrative is

   A. La Salle Meets his Brother
   B. New France
   C. La Salle Claims Louisiana Territory
   D. Native Americans and La Salle

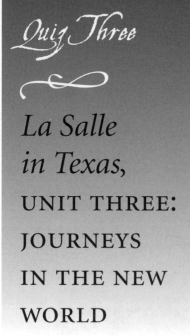

Quiz Three

La Salle in Texas,

UNIT THREE:

JOURNEYS

IN THE NEW

WORLD

3. La Salle's trip down the Mississippi River in 1682 . . .

    A. upset the Native Americans.
    B. surprised the British on the east coast.
    C. established French claim to the Louisiana territory.
    D. took ten years.

4. The French explorer, La Salle, wanted to establish a fort and trading post . . .

    A. in Cuba.
    B. at the mouth of the Mississippi River.
    C. in Florida.
    D. on the Rio Grande River.

Use the information in the box below and your knowledge of social studies to answer the following:

> Establishing a trading post at the mouth of the Mississippi River would accomplish many objectives for France and King Louis XIV.

5. Which of the following would NOT result if the trading post were set up?

    A. France could control vast territory along the river.
    B. Explorers in the Gulf of Mexico could get supplies easily.
    C. France could learn more about what Spain was doing.
    D. The English could have more active spies.

> During the 1600s the ports in the West Indies were used by many countries as a stopover.

6. Which of the following was NOT true?

    A. They loaded on supplies.
    B. They made repairs to their ships.
    C. They went to the bank for more money.
    D. They got fresh water and fruit.

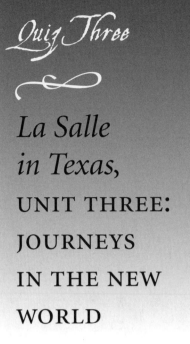

Quiz Three

La Salle in Texas,

UNIT THREE:

JOURNEYS

IN THE NEW

WORLD

7. When *La Belle* sank in the storm, La Salle secured Fort St. Louis and then . . .

    A. went to Mexico (called New Spain at the time).
    B. traveled on foot into east Texas.
    C. sailed to France.
    D. canoed up the Mississippi River.

8. After La Salle and his party left Fort St. Louis, the people in the fort . . .

    A. greeted a wagon train with supplies.
    B. harvested crops.
    C. were massacred and the fort was burned.
    D. got supplies by ship from France.

Use the information in the box below and your knowledge of social studies to answer question 9

> Events in the Life of La Salle
> 1666 La Salle traveled to New France (Canada).
> 1682 La Salle claimed territory drained by Mississippi River for France.
> 1684 ??
> 1686 *La Belle* sank during a storm.
> 1687 La Salle was ambushed and killed by his men.

9. Which of the following events completes the timeline above?

    A. La Salle sailed from France with four ships.
    B. La Salle was born in France.
    C. La Salle built trading posts in New France.
    D. Joutel and five men return to France.

10. La Salle's effort to establish a settlement is typical of the . . .

    A. Middle Ages.
    B. Scientific Revolution.
    C. Origin of Civilization.
    D. Age of Exploration and Colonization.

Unit Four

SURVIVNG ALONG THE GULF COAST: CULTURAL ADAPTATION

Overview

Unit Summary: Students will create displays and charts of five cultures for comparison.

ENDURING UNDERSTANDINGS

Indigenous people react to newcomers in a variety of ways.

People who migrate take their culture and knowledge with them.

Respect of cultural differences is important in a pluralistic society.

ESSENTIAL QUESTIONS

What can we learn by studying past cultures?

What do artifacts tell us about how people lived?

How do cultural traits diffuse?

In what ways does culture continue and change with migration?

How did cultures adapt to the environment?

Why do people migrate?

What was one culture's reaction to the other cultures; for example, how did the Karankawa react to the French?

How can we include the voices of all Americans in our national history?

SOCIAL STUDIES STRANDS— NATIONAL COUNCIL FOR SOCIAL STUDIES

Culture (French, Karankawa, Caddo, Spanish, Jumano)

Time, Continuity, and Change (prehistoric, historic, colonial)

Production, Distribution, and Consumption (subsistence, trade, colonial)

Science, Technology, and Society (prehistoric technology, archeological techniques)

CURRICULUM STANDARDS FOR SOCIAL STUDIES — NATIONAL COUNCIL FOR SOCIAL STUDIES

Name the common characteristics of different cultures.

List how people meet their basic needs in a variety of contexts.

Compare similarities and differences in the ways groups meet human needs and concerns.

Explain why individuals and groups respond differently to their physical and social environments on the basis of shared assumptions, values and beliefs.

Explain how information and

experiences may be interpreted differently by people from diverse cultural perspectives and frames of reference.

TEKS:

4.2, 4.4, 4.6, 4.8, 4.9, 4.10, 4.11, 4.20, 4.22, 4.23, 4.24

5.1, 5.6, 5.9, 5.10, 5.11, 5.25, 5.26, 5.27

6.2, 6.3, 6.7, 6.8, 6.14, 6.15, 6.16, 6.21, 6.22, 6.23

7.1, 7.2, 7.12, 7.16, 7.27, 7.23, 7.28

8.1, 8.2, 8.10, 8.11, 8.20, 8.24, 8.30, 8.31, 8.32

Getting Started

Levels: grades 4–8

Subjects: social studies, science, technology, language arts, visual arts, math

Skills: critical thinking skills to organize and use information acquired from a variety of sources including electronic technology; communication skills for written, oral, and visual forms; problem-solving and decision-making skills, working independently and with others in a variety of settings.

Time: five 45–60 minute class periods

Class size: any number of students divided into five groups for study and presentation (display)

RESOURCES FOR UNIT *principal resources for this unit in **bold**

Books

*Bruseth, James E. and Toni S. Turner. *From a Watery Grave: The Discovery and Excavation of La Salle's Shipwreck,* La Belle.* College Station: Texas A&M University Press, 2005 (referred to as *FWG*). Adult to intermediate level. A detailed account of the recovery of *La Belle*. Many photographs and illustrations. Some primary accounts are quoted. Excellent bibliography.

Audiovisuals

Dreams of Conquest. Alan Govenar, Documentary Arts, 2004. Details of the story of La Salle, from his boyhood in France to exploration in the New World. *Please observe content advisory for this DVD. See Guides to DVDs, p. 111, for detailed summary.*

Internet Connections — Using Technology

www.tsha.utexas.edu/handbook/on-line/ Handbook of Texas from Texas State Historical Association

www.texasbeyondhistory.net/timberhill/index.html Information on historic Caddo culture.

www.texasbeyondhistory.net/belle/lesson.html Lesson on The French in Texas.

www.thc.state.tx.us Texas Historical Commission. State agency for historic preservation

www.texas-settlement.org/ Texas Settlement Region — La Salle Odyssey museums

www.texancultures.utsa.edu Institute of Texan Cultures resources.

www.lsjunction.com Lone Star Junction, a Texas history resource

www.nativeculture.com Links to homepages for Native American nations/tribes

www.caddonation-nsn.gov/ Web site created by the Caddo people, filled with details on history, language, art and music.

www.tpwd.state.tx.us/park/caddoan State park for Caddoan Mounds.

www.utexas.edu/research/tarl/current.html Includes information on excavation in Caddo region.

MATERIALS AND EQUIPMENT NEEDED

5 Spaces for display — (one for each group) one poster board plus three shoe boxes for artifacts

Materials to create displays: 5 poster boards, 15 shoe boxes, white paper, colored paper, markers, glue sticks

INSTRUCTIONS FOR STUDENTS for each group

NOTES ABOUT CULTURES for each specific group

Access to computer for exhibit labels

CULTURES IN TEXAS 1685–1725 chart, copy for each student

Internet access for technology connections

Content Brief

When Robert Cavelier, Sieur de la Salle, landed on the present-day Texas coast in 1684, the area was populated by Native Americans who had been there for thousands of years. The first group La Salle saw was a band of the *Karankawa* along the shore. La Salle and his colonists brought *French* customs to the coast as they established Fort St. Louis. After the colony got started, La Salle made reconnaissance trips that lasted several months, searching for the Mississippi River. In these travels,

La Salle encountered the *Caddo* in present-day east Texas. At this same time, the *Spanish* had mission complexes in northern Mexico and in the early 1700s established missions and presidios in present-day Texas. The *Jumano* were Indian traders who reported the presence of the French to the Spanish. The Jumano lived along the Concho River in west central Texas and traveled frequently to the Rio Grande River.

Each of these cultures adapted to the environment in ways familiar to themselves but different from their contemporaries. They met their basic needs for shelter, food, tools, weapons, law and order, and religion in ways that reflected their cultural traditions.

See NOTES ABOUT CULTURES (STUDENT PAGES) for more details and references.

VOCABULARY

Word bank for notebook or word wall for easy reference. Additional vocabulary is defined in the glossary.

Caddo: Native Americans who lived in East Texas woodlands

Culture: way of life, patterns for living

Jumano: Native Americans who lived in Central West Texas along the Concho River

Karankawa: Native Americans who lived along the Gulf coast

Subsistence: that which furnishes support for life; to be maintained with food and clothing

UNIT STRUCTURE: W.H.E.R.E.

Where is this lesson going; Hook students with interesting information; Explore the details of the history and enable the student to learn; Reflect on new learning; Evaluate and assess student learning during the lesson.

WHERE

Student groups will produce displays that show similarities and differences between (1) the French settlers, (2) the Karankawa, (3) the Jumano, (4) the Caddo, and (5) the Spanish. These displays will answer questions posed in Facets of Understanding.

Students will record information on the comparative chart CULTURES IN TEXAS 1650–1750 by viewing the displays. They will also answer the question: How can we include the voices of all Americans in our national history?

HOOK

Class 1: Ask students:

If you were dropped/abandoned on a tropical island, what would you need to survive?

How would you get shelter, food, and tools?

What rules would you want? Who would be the leader?

How long could you live without contact with the world you left?

EXPLORE

Class 1: Use INTRODUCTION to Unit Four.

Class 2: Students will continue assignment.

Class 3: Students will complete the display.

Class 4: Student tour guides will present their commentaries about their displays for the class. Students use information to complete the comparative chart of CULTURES IN TEXAS 1650–1750. (If possible, arrange for other audiences — younger students, parents, et. al. — to view the displays and presentations.)

Class 5: Students complete CULTURES IN TEXAS 1650–1750 and answer the question: How can we include the voices of all Americans in our national history?

REFLECT

Student groups will create interpretive labels for the displays that explain the ways the cultures provided for basic human needs.

Each individual student will complete a comparative chart of CULTURES IN TEXAS 1650–1750 based on display and presentations by groups.

They will also answer the question: How can we include the voices of all Americans in our national history?

EVALUATE

Rubrics provided under Standards section in Performance Tasks.

(group) Students will set up displays and conduct tours.

(individual) Each student will complete the chart CULTURES IN TEXAS 1650–1750 and answer the question: How can we include the voices of all Americans in our national history in discussion or essay?

Introduction to Unit Four: Surviving along the Gulf Coast

Review basic information with the students.

People who settled in new regions often use survivor techniques when they first arrive.

When La Salle came to the coast of Texas in the 1680s, he and the colonists brought the French culture with them. Their first few months on the coast were difficult. The first group they encountered on shore were the Karankawa, who lived from resources along the coast: fish, oysters, and clams. During La Salle's travels he traded with the Caddo people. They lived in villages and farmed. The Spanish were looking for La Salle and later settled on the land occupied by Fort St. Louis. Spanish missions at this time were located along the Rio Grande and not yet in Texas. The Jumano also traded with the French and Spanish. They lived in villages along the Concho River in West Central Texas, but traveled a lot.

Students will review historic and archeological evidence telling how each of these cultures survived along the Texas coast in 1650–1750.

Divide students into five groups. Have each group pick (or assign) a culture to research: Karankawa, French, Caddo, Spanish, or Jumano.

Remind students to learn as much as they can about how each specific culture lived in 1650–1750.

One way to study a culture is to look at how people satisfy their basic needs of shelter, clothing, food, water, law and order, and beliefs (religion). Supply NOTES ABOUT CULTURES and INSTRUCTIONS FOR STUDENTS to each group. Each group will design a display that relates information about the assigned culture group.

Say to students: Consider how this might work if we did a display about our classroom culture. Where do you live? (sketch map of neighborhood) What do you eat? (artifactual trash from fast food or home pantry) Do we have rules? (posted rules or code of conduct) What other things would describe the class culture?

Ask students to apply those ideas to their assigned culture. Remind them to work together using the NOTES ABOUT CULTURES to complete their assigned culture on the chart CULTURES IN TEXAS. They should also use the chart and other information to develop a display.

Displays should include the following:
1) A map that shows where the culture settled. Map should have title, key, compass rose, and scale.
2) Many artifacts that relate how the culture met its basic needs of shelter, clothing, food, water, law and order, and beliefs or religion
3) Labels for the display that enable people to understand that culture's adaptation to Texas.
4) Visuals that are colorful, neat, and easy to read.

5) Answers to these questions from Facets of Understanding in the display:
    In what ways does culture continue/change with migration?
    How did cultures adapt or alter the environment to suit their needs?
    Why do some people migrate?
    What was one culture's reaction to the other cultures on the Texas coast?

Provide books, DVD, and access to Internet from the RESOURCES list. Provide a defined space and materials from which to create the display of maps, illustrations, and artifacts. Displays should have one poster board for the map and introduction and three shoe boxes for artifacts.

Assist students as needed with INSTRUCTIONS FOR STUDENTS and NOTES ABOUT CULTURES.

Facets of Understanding integrated into unit:

Explanation: In what ways does culture continue/change with migration? How did cultures adapt or alter the environment to suit their needs?
Interpretation: Why do some people/cultures migrate?
Perspective: What was one culture's reaction to the others?
Application: What can we do to include the voices of all Americans

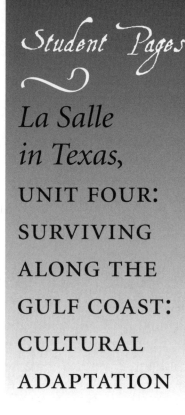

La Salle
in Texas,
UNIT FOUR:
SURVIVING
ALONG THE
GULF COAST:
CULTURAL
ADAPTATION

in our national history?
INSTRUCTIONS FOR STUDENTS (one copy per group)

Your display (one poster board and three shoe boxes) should include the following:
1) A map that shows where the culture settled. Map should have title, key, compass rose, and scale.
2) Many artifacts that relate how the culture met its basic needs of shelter, clothing, food, water, law and order, and beliefs or religion.
3) Labels for the display that enable people to understand that culture's adaptation to the environment.
4) Visuals that are colorful, neat, and easy to read.
5) Answers to these questions from Facets of Understanding in the display:
   In what ways does culture continue/change with migration?
   How did cultures adapt or alter the environment to suit their needs?
   Why do some people/cultures migrate?
   What was one culture's reaction to the other cultures on the Texas coast?

Roles: You will choose one role for your group.

_____ Curator: organize display, create labels for general topics.

_____ Researcher: answer questions from Facets of Understanding (above).

_____ Cartographer: find or draw map of where the culture was located; map should have title, key, north arrow and scale.

_____ Artist: draw or find other illustrations about the culture.

_____ Docent (tour guide): give a talk about display.

Tasks: You will prepare at least one part of the display by creating or finding artifacts and writing labels.

_____ shelter   _____ weapons

_____ clothing   _____ law and order

_____ food/economy   _____ beliefs/religion

_____ tools

GROUP ONE — THE FRENCH: NOTES ABOUT CULTURES

Sources for information
Bruseth, *From a Watery Grave* (*FWG*), pp. 8, 17, 21–22, 27, 104–5
Weddle, *The French Thorn*
Foster, *The La Salle Expedition in Texas*
www.texasbeyondhistory.net/belle/lesson.html
www.thc.state.tx.us
www.tsha.utexas.edu/handbook/online

Fort St. Louis and *La Belle* tell us many things about the French who came to Texas in the late 1600s. Archeologists who uncovered the story of the French also inspired historians and geographers to revisit the research and documents about La Salle and his colony. This renewed interest in the French began to complete the picture of this early European settlement along the Gulf coast.

Fort St. Louis was more of an outpost than a true fort. The French built a main building: two stories with four rooms—three downstairs and one upstairs. La Salle, the officers, and the clergy occupied the rooms. Upstairs was the storeroom. See illustration (*FWG* p. 8) and read about the building (*FWG* p. 104–5). A map was made by the Spanish military expedition who found the outpost in 1689 (*FWG* p. 27).

From this map, we know that eight iron cannons protected the fort. These iron cannons were excavated in 1997 by archeologists from the Texas Historical Commission. (*FWG* pp. 28, 93) The French also had muskets (*FWG* p. 94) and a verso (swivel gun) on the ship. There were pole arms (*FWG* p. 98) and a lot of ammunition (*FWG* p. 95). The French colony also had a crucible for melting lead to make bullets.

We know from artifacts found on *La Belle* and later at Fort St. Louis that the French brought many items to set up their houses. They brought grinding stones for making flour or corn meal (*FWG* p. 103), and cooking equipment such as a colander and copper pots. The archeologists found many spoons and a few forks (*FWG* p. 102). Stoneware and earthenware (*FWG* pp. 98–99), pewter plates and cups, and glass bottles (*FWG* p. 101) demonstrate how well prepared they were.

Tools were packed in barrels that included axe heads (*FWG* p. 91), knives (*FWG* p. 91), carpentry tools (*FWG* p. 104), rope, and copper wire.

In order to survive on the frontier, the colonists brought seed to plant. Unfortunately, they did not have a very good harvest. They brought some animals with them—pigs, cattle, goats, chickens, and dogs—and they were able to kill game—bison and deer. They also caught fish and turtles (*FWG* p. 123). Their diet seems to have been good, based on the bones found by archeologists. One other critter that they apparently ate was the opossum (*FWG* p. 127).

Personal items were also found among the cargo on *La Belle*. These included shoes, pipes, and religious items: rosary beads and a cross. Finger rings that have religious symbols on them (*FWG* p. 209) were probably for gifts. Small brass bells were also for trade. Gaming pieces like dice were also excavated. Clothing of the time period can be seen in illustrations (*FWG* pp. 17, 21, 22).

The expedition was led and governed by La Salle and whomever he appointed.

We know a great deal about the French colony from the diary of Henri Joutel (*FWG* p. 29), who returned to France and published his journal.

GROUP TWO — THE KARANKAWA: NOTES ABOUT CULTURES

Student Pages

La Salle
in Texas,
UNIT FOUR:
SURVIVING
ALONG THE
GULF COAST:
CULTURAL
ADAPTATION

Sources of information
Bruseth, *From a Watery Grave (FWG)*, pp. 3–5, 16, 25–26
www.tsha.utexas.edu/handbook/online
Ricklis, *The Karankawa*
Foster, *The La Salle Expedition to Texas*
Weddle, *La Salle, the Mississippi, and the Gulf*

The Karankawa lived along the Texas coast and reportedly were large men (6'6"). Women were smaller (5'4"). They tattooed, pierced, and painted their bodies. Women wore grass and moss garments and skins in winter. Historic accounts relate stories of cannibalism but no archeological evidence of this has been found.

Karankawa fed the tribe by hunting, fishing, and gathering. (*FWG* p. 4). They harvested many oysters and clams and created large middens when they discarded the shells. They also ate deer, an occasional bison, and cattail roots for starch.

The men carried large cedar bows that came up to eye level.

Karankawa lived in shelters made of poles covered by skins or bark, referred to as Ba-ak, that housed 7–9 people. They lived and traveled in bands of 30–40, with a chief in charge. They also had dugout canoes large enough to hold a family and all its goods.

They made baskets from reeds and pottery from local clay.

They celebrated with ceremonies including dancing, contests, and games.

The French colonists encountered Karankawa on arrival (*FWG* pp. 4, 25–26 and 16). Due to blundering by La Salle's men, who stole some of the tribe's canoes, the Karankawa became hostile and were a threat to the colonists. They reportedly killed sailors (*FWG* pp. 3, 5) and, when defenses were down at Fort St. Louis, the Karankawa massacred the settlers in the winter of 1689. They did, however, adopt several children to whom they were reportedly kind.

Student Page

La Salle in Texas,

UNIT FOUR:
SURVIVNG
ALONG THE
GULF COAST:
CULTURAL
ADAPTATION

Sources of information
Bruseth, *From a Watery Grave* (*FWG*), pp. 28–29, 87–89
www.texasbeyondhistory.net/tejas
www.texasbeyondhistory.net/timberhill/index
Foster, *The La Salle Expedition to Texas*
Perttula, *The Caddo Nation*
Carter, *Caddo Indians*
www.caddonation-nsn.gov/
www.tpwd.state.tx.us/park/caddoan Caddoan Mounds State Park
www.tsha.utexas.edu/handbook/online

The Caddo whom the French encountered had been in East Texas for thousands of years. The French called one band the "Cenis." The Spanish called them "Tejas" and they called themselves "Hasinai."

The Caddo lived in villages of beehive-shaped houses (*FWG* p. 29). Their villages were in river and stream valleys and often were not stockaded. A chief, who also served as religious leader, ruled the people. They had ritual centers with temples, built on mounds.

They were skilled farmers who grew corn, beans, squash, and sunflowers. They also hunted deer and small game.

The Caddo were known as skilled potters. They made lovely jars, bowls, pipes, and ear spools.

La Salle made numerous references to the Caddo with whom he actively traded (*FWG* p. 87–88). The French had many items that the Caddo wanted: axes, knives, needles, kettles, and beads (*FWG* p. 10). The French, in turn, wanted horses and food that the Caddo could supply (*FWG* p. 28). One documented exchange was four needles for a fully dressed deer hide (*FWG* p. 89); another trade was one axe head for a horse.

The Caddo tribe moved many times as settlers came into Texas. About 4,000 Caddo live today in Oklahoma, near Binger.

La Salle in Texas, UNIT FOUR: SURVIVING ALONG THE GULF COAST: CULTURAL ADAPTATION

Sources of information
Bruseth, *From A Watery Grave* (*FWG*), pp. 6–10, 34–35
Chipman, *Explorers and Settlers of Spanish Texas*
www.tsha.utexas.edu/handbook/online

At the time of La Salle, the Spanish had outposts on the Rio Grande River at Presidio and El Paso. They had not been active in the territory that became Texas. But when they received reports from the Jumano in 1687 about the French along the Gulf coast they sent 11 expeditions to find them — several traveled overland and several by sea (*FWG* pp. 6–10). As early as April, 1687, members of the Rivas y Yriarte expedition spotted the wreck of *La Belle* and named it "Navio Quebrado" ("Broken Ship"). They did not realize that La Salle and his colonists were living on Garcitas Creek at the time.

In April 1689, the De Leon expedition found the remains of settlers who were killed by the Karankawa in the winter of 1688–89. Spanish maps were drawn to record the French settlement and ship (*FWG* pp. 34–35).

The Spanish understood that they needed to establish a stronger presence to protect their interests in Texas. In April 1721, the Spanish began building the Presidio La Bahia on the same location as Fort St. Louis. By 1722 they also had Mission Espiritu Santo, across Garcitas Creek. The Franciscans established this mission. Their goal was to establish autonomous church-towns to serve the Native Americans and colonists moving from Mexico and Spain.

The mission had a routine daily life of prayer, work, training, meals, and relaxation. The mission usually had walls for protection, rooms for the clergy, guards, and Native Americans. Most soldiers were housed in the presidio. Often a well was dug inside the mission. Fields for agriculture and pastures for stock were outside the walls.

The Native Americans were given simple cotton clothing (shirt and trousers, tunic dress) to wear. The Franciscan friars wore their traditional robes. The military had uniforms issued by the Spanish government in Mexico.

Objects that tell us about daily life in the mission include pottery, metal tools, and weapons. Religious items included vessels and decorations for the chapel, medals and rosaries for the friars, and some religious tokens for the Native Americans.

The physical structures for Presidio La Bahia and Mission Espiritu Santo were moved several times: 1722 on Garcitas Creek, 1726–36 at two locations on the Guadalupe, 1749 on the San Antonio River, where the mission is showcased today at Goliad State Park, with Presido La Bahia adjacent.

Student Pages

La Salle in Texas,

UNIT FOUR:
SURVIVING
ALONG THE
GULF COAST:
CULTURAL
ADAPTATION

Sources of information
Bruseth, *From a Watery Grave* (*FWG*) pp. 9–12
www.tsha.utexas.edu/handbook/online
Kenmotsu, *Seeking Friends, Avoiding Enemies*

The Jumano were a band of Native Americans whose homelands were on the Concho River in west central Texas. They often visited the pueblos of New Mexico and the rancherias near the Rio Grande. At different times they lived in pueblos, dug-out houses and sometimes, tipis.

The Jumano lived in extended family households. They hunted bison (when available), gathered plants, and farmed in a limited way. They grew squash and melons. They gathered prickly pear and caught fish in nearby rivers.

When traveling, they lived in skin-covered tipis. They rode horses (after the Spanish came to North America in the 1500s) and hunted bison with bows and arrows. Archeological sites identified with the Jumano contain Perdiz arrow points, chert knives, scrapers, drills, and pottery with an interior wash.

The men wore short hair and the women wore braids. They wore loose garments of tanned skins. Jumano had distinctive facial markings of horizontal lines or bands. (*FWG* p. 12)

Jumano were well known for being traders and traveled great distances to deliver goods and messages. As early as 1583, the Spanish visited them on the Pecos River. In 1629 some 80,000 "souls" were reported as converted to Christianity. In 1650 the Spanish were guests of the Jumano for six months on the Rio de las Nueces. The Jumano were stressed in the mid-1600s when a drought caused the bison herds to move north. (Kenmotsu p. 28) They sought a close association with the Spanish, who appeared stronger and more powerful with their guns and horses.

In 1682 Jumano leader Juan Sabeata visited the Spanish in El Paso to encourage an alliance whereby the Jumano would introduce the Spanish to other Indian groups. In 1687 the Jumano reported to the Spanish that they had seen "Moors" who lived in wooden houses on the water: likely the French on *La Belle* (*FWG* p. 10). In 1688, the Jumano convinced the Spanish general Retana to travel to their homeland in west central Texas. (Kenmotsu, p. 32). In 1689 several Jumano chiefs delivered pages of the log of *La Belle* to Spanish Governor Pardinas in Nueva Vizcaya (northern Mexico), which further alerted the Spanish to the French colonists (*FWG* p. 9). The Jumano hoped to maintain a close association with the Spanish to be protected against their mutual enemies, the Apache.

But by the 1700s the Spanish were more interested in silver in Chihuahua, settlements in New Mexico, and the threat from the French in east Texas than central Texas. The Jumano formed a new alliance with the Apache against a still bigger threat: the Comanche (Kenmotsu, p. 33).

PERFORMANCE TASKS: G.R.A.S.P.S. (copy for each group)
The acronym G.R.A.S.P.S. stands for **Goal**, **Role**, **Audience**, **Situation**, **Product**, **Standards**.

Goals
You will learn about five cultures that were active in Texas in 1650–1750.

Role
You will have one role on the team: Curator — organize display; Researcher — answer questions from Facets of Understanding; Cartographer — find or draw map of where the culture was located; Artist — draw or find illustrations about the culture; Docent (tour guide) — give a talk about display
You will also prepare part of the display to show how the culture met its basic needs.

Audience
You will present information to your class so individual students may complete the comparative chart CULTURES IN TEXAS 1650–1750.

Situation
If possible, invite a younger class to take a tour of the displays. Practice the tour presentations for the class in advance.

Product
(*Group*) display and tour
(*Individual*) chart of CULTURES IN TEXAS 1650–1750 and the answer for the following question: How can we include the voices of all Americans in our national history.

Standards — Assessment

RUBRICS
Students may create criteria for evaluation or use the following.

For group culture display with tour:
Level 4 (highest)
The group's map shows where the culture settled. Map should have title, key, north arrow (compass rose), and scale.
Many artifacts relate how the culture met its basic needs (seven categories).
Labels for the display enable people to understand that culture's adaptation to Texas.
The display is colorful, neat, and easy to read.
The display answers three (3) questions from Facets of Understanding in the display.

Student Page

La Salle in Texas,

UNIT FOUR:
SURVIVING
ALONG THE
GULF COAST:
CULTURAL
ADAPTATION

La Salle in Texas,

UNIT FOUR: SURVIVING ALONG THE GULF COAST: CULTURAL ADAPTATION

Level 3

The map shows little detail where the culture settled. Map has only a few components.

Some artifacts relate how the culture met its basic needs (at least five categories).

Labels for the display relate some of the culture's adaptation to Texas.

The display is colorful.

The display answers two (2) Facets of Understanding in the display.

Level 2

The map shows where the culture settled. Map has only a few components.

A few artifacts relate how the culture met its basic needs (at least three categories).

Labels for the display relate a little about culture's adaptation to Texas.

The display is plain.

Incorporates one (1) Facet of Understanding into the display.

Level 1

No map.

Few artifacts relate how the culture met its basic needs (one or no categories).

Labels tell little about the culture's adaptation to Texas.

The display is dull, messy, and not easy to read.

Incorporates no Facets of Understanding.

For individual students' comparative chart of CULTURES IN TEXAS 1650–1750:

Complete the chart to show how cultures met their basic needs (35 blocks of information). Answers should be brief but accurate.

Level 4 (highest): Complete 35 blocks of information on the chart.

Level 3: Complete 34–24 blocks of information.

Level 2: Complete 23–13 blocks of information.

Level 1: Complete 12 or fewer blocks of information.

Discussion or essay:

Answer the following question from Facets of Understanding: How can we include the voices of all Americans in our national history?

Level 4 (highest): Answer the question from Facets of Understanding with 3–5 complete sentences.

Level 3: Answer question from Facets of Understanding with 2 complete sentences.

Level 2: Answer question from Facets of Understanding with 1 sentence.

Level 1: Does not answer question from Facets of Understanding.

Extend across the Curriculum

VISUAL ARTS

1) Create a poster or brochure to advertise the La Salle Odyssey trail.

Seven museums are included in the La Salle Odyssey trail:

Corpus Christi Museum of Science and History (Corpus Christi) www.ccmuseum.com

Texas Maritime Museum (Rockport) www.texasmaritimemuseum.org

Texana Museum (Edna) (at time of press it did not have a web site)

Calhoun County Museum (Port Lavaca) www.calhouncountymuseum.org

Museum of the Coastal Bend (Victoria) www.museumofthecoastalbend.org

Matagorda County Museum (Bay City) www.matagordacountymuseum.org

La Petite Belle Homeport (Palacios) www.palaciosmuseum.org

2) Find information on the regalia and dances of Native American tribes near you. If possible, visit and participate in a Powwow. Tell your class about your experience.

GEOGRAPHY

1) Locate a map that shows Native American tribes today. Which ones do you have in your state?

2) How do the different topographic zones relate to the adaptation by the early cultures?

3) When thinking about how the early people traveled, we need to remember that the rivers (and valleys) were like highways.

Compare distance by river and by highway from San Antonio to Seadrift; from Dallas to Anahuac; others.

MATH

1) LaSalle and his men traveled from Fort St. Louis to the Caddo villages (near Nacogdoches) to trade. Determine how many miles that trip would be. _____ (approx. 325 miles). If they walked 15 miles a day, how many days would that trip take? _____ (16).

2) The Jumano were messengers and traders for the Spanish. They traveled from near Presidio to El Paso to tell the Spanish about the French fort on the coast. How far was that journey? _____ (approx. 200 miles). If they traveled 15 miles a day, how long would it take them? _____ (13).

LANGUAGE ARTS

1) Write a journal as if you were a member of one of the cultures represented. See "The French in Texas" lesson at www.texasbeyondhistory.net/belle/lesson.html.

2) Find a record of Native American languages. Create a story using another language.

Your name	CULTURES IN TEXAS 1650–1750				Page 1
	KARANKAWA	FRENCH	CADDO	SPANISH	JUMANO
Shelter Ex. tent					
Clothing Ex. shirt					
Food/ Economy Ex. farm					
Tools Ex. axe					

Your name	CULTURES IN TEXAS 1650–1750				Page 2
	KARANKAWA	FRENCH	CADDO	SPANISH	JUMANO
Weapons Ex. musket					
Law and order Ex. chief					
Beliefs/ Religion Ex. Catholic					
Other					

Answer this question in discussion or essay:
How can we include the voices of all Americans in our national history?

KEY	CULTURES IN TEXAS 1650–1750				
	Karankawa	French	Caddo	Spanish	Jumano
Shelter	Ba-ak — poles covered with skins or branches	Fort with 2 story bldg., other small cabins	Large beehive houses — sleeping room for 10	Masonry mission complex	Tipis when travelling; sometimes adobe in pueblo
Clothing	Tanned hides, grass & moss	Brought from France	Tanned hides, later traded for cotton	From Spain or Mexico — uniform or robes	Garments of tanned skins; men — short hair; women — braids; facial markings
Food/ economy	Oysters, clams, fish, turtle, deer, roots Subsistence economy	Pig, cattle, goat, chicken, deer, bison, opossum Craft specialization economy	Corn, bean, squash, sunflower seeds, game Agricultural economy	Corn, wheat, goat, cattle, game, fish Craft specialization economy	Mixed economy — Corn, squash, melons, prickly pear tunas, bison, fish
Tools	Bow and arrow; pottery, baskets	Axes, grinding stones, dishes, pots	Jars, bowls, pipes, knives, needles	Pottery, metal tools	Bow and arrows, knives, scrapers, drills, pottery
Weapons	Bow and arrow	8 cannon, swivel gun, muskets	Bow and arrows, some muskets	muskets	Bow and Perdiz arrows
Law and order	Tribal	La Salle was in charge and appointed a commander when away	Chief with council — also religious leader	commandant of military in presidio; friar in church	Numerous chiefs
Beliefs/ Religion	Ceremonies	Catholic	Temples on mounds	Catholic	Invited missionaries to visit; adopted Christian symbols to please Spanish
Other	No evidence of cannibalism		Still identifiable tribe	La Bahia	Major traders across the plains and pueblos

STUDENT NAME _____ DATE _____

Quiz Four

*La Salle
in Texas,*
UNIT FOUR:
SURVIVING
ALONG THE
GULF COAST:
CULTURAL
ADAPTATION

Use information in the box and your knowledge of social studies to answer question 1

> Cultural characteristics:
> Shelter
> Clothing
> Food
> Law and order
> Beliefs

1. What characteristic fits in the list above?

   A. Tools and technology
   B. Songs
   C. Elections
   D. Slogans

The French who came to Texas with La Salle brought many household items.

2. What items were NOT brought from France?

   A. Grinding stones
   B. Copper pots
   C. Oven for baking
   D. Pewter plates and cups

3. We learn about the French from a primary source: a published diary written by . . .

   A. Henri Joutel
   B. Sieur de La Salle
   C. Henri Mallet
   D. Father Marquette

4. Fort St. Louis was an outpost with . . .

   A. a stone wall around it.
   B. a main building with two stories.
   C. a dock for ships to land.
   D. successful crops.

La Salle in Texas,

UNIT FOUR: SURVIVING ALONG THE GULF COAST: CULTURAL ADAPTATION

5. This tribe survived primarily by harvesting shellfish from the bays. Who were they?

    A. Jumano
    B. Karankawa
    C. Caddo
    D. Comanche

Use information in the box and your knowledge of social studies to answer question 6

> *French Trade Items that the Caddo Liked*
> Pins
> Axes
> Hawk bells

6. Which of the following items would also fit in this list above?

    A. Corn
    B. Horses
    C. Glass beads
    D. Deer hide

7. At the time of La Salle, the Spanish had settlements . . .

    A. along the Rio Grande
    B. along the Guadalupe River
    C. on Padre Island
    D. along the Red River

Use information in the box and your knowledge of social studies to answer question 8

> *Title?*
> To keep other Europeans out
> To find gold and silver
> To Christianize the Native Americans

8. The best title for this list is

    A. Reasons Mexico fought Texas
    B. Reasons the Spanish settled Texas
    C. Reasons the Texians fought Mexico
    D. Why colonists moved to Texas

9. This tribe was known for being active traders of goods and information in the 1600s. What was its name?

    A. Comanche
    B. Jumano
    C. Seminole
    D. Karankawa

Use information in the box and your knowledge of social studies to answer quwstion 10

> From a French explorer's diary: "I asked him (one of the Caddo) by signs if he wanted to exchange a deer hide for a few needles. I showed him two and demonstrated the purpose they served. I gave him two more needles (to complete the trade — four needles for one deer hide)."

10. The best title for this excerpt would be

    A. Trade with Spanish
    B. Needles Were Valuable Trade Items
    C. French Wanted Hides for Shoes
    D. Traveling with La Salle

Quiz Four

La Salle in Texas,

UNIT FOUR:
SURVIVING
ALONG THE
GULF COAST:
CULTURAL
ADAPTATION

The story of the La Salle expedition seems to end with the wreck of *La Belle* and the death of La Salle but, in fact, some of the people were resilient and their descendants are alive today. The number of people involved in the expedition is uncertain, as many remained unnamed. Gilmore is able to account for 91 settlers and an indefinite number of sailors, many of whom stayed with the colony.

After La Salle's murder, arguments among that band of men resulted in several more deaths. Eventually Henri Joutel, Abbé Jean Cavelier (La Salle's brother), Colin Cavelier (La Salle's nephew), and Father Anastase Douy returned to France. Joutel married upon his return to France and wrote about his experience in a published journal. Colin Cavelier became a soldier but died shortly after his return to France. Father Douay returned to the Gulf Coast with Iberville, who founded Mobile.

Several men including Jean L'Archeveque and Jacques Grollet stayed with the Caddo Indians after La Salle's death. They were captured by the Spanish and were sent to New Mexico for colonization with Vargas in 1693. Grollet married and had a

son named Antonio Gurule whose descendants live primarily in the southwest. Grollet changed his family name to Santiago Gurule, and L'Archeveque became Archibeque, both more Hispanic-sounding names. L'Archeveque (Archibeque) also has descendants scattered over the southwest. Pierre Meunier was another member of the expedition who was sent to New Mexico after the De Leon expedition located him. Meunier married a daughter of a soldier in El Paso del Norte, but little else is known about him.

Members of the Talon family were colonists who relocated from Canada to Texas with La Salle. They brought six children with them. The father, Lucien, was lost on an exploring trip. The mother, Isabelle Planteau Talon, was killed in the Fort St. Louis massacre in 1688. The eldest daughter, Marie Elizabeth, died during the winter of 1685–86. Pierre was left by La Salle with the Caddo Indians to learn their language. Marie-Madaline, Jean-Baptiste, Lucien, Robert, and Eustace Breman (another child with the Talon family) were saved by the Karankawa women from the 1688 massacre.

The Talon children and Meunier were collected from the Caddo and

105

Karankawa by the De Leon expedition in 1690 and sent to Mexico. The Talon brothers returned to France and their sister went to Canada. Pierre and Robert later accompanied the second expedition by Iberville to the Gulf Coast. Robert Talon resided in Mobile, where his descendants live today.

References

Bruseth, James E. and Toni S. Turner. *From A Watery Grave: The Discovery and Excavation of La Salle's Shipwreck,* La Belle. College Station: Texas A&M University Press, 2005.

Foster, William C., ed. *Save the Young: The 1691 Expedition of Captain Martinez to Rescue the Last Survivors of the Massacre at Fort St. Louis, Texas.* Corpus Christi: American Binding and Printing, 2004. Available from the Museum of the Coastal Bend, Victoria.

Gilmore, Kathleen K. "Treachery and Tragedy in the Texas Wilderness: The Adventures of Jean L'Archeveque in Texas." *Bulletin of the Texas Archeological Society,* Volume 69, pp. 35–46 (with King H. Gill). Austin: Texas Archeological Society, 1998.

Gilmore, Kathleen. "People of La Salle's Last Expedition," *Bulletin of the Texas Archeological Society,* Volume 76, pp.107–121. Austin: Texas Archeological Society, 2005.

Weddle, R. S. "La Salle's Survivors." *Southwest Historical Quarterly* Vol. 75(4). Austin: Texas State Historical Association, 1972.

The Shipwreck of La Belle is a fast moving film about the discovery and recovery of the shipwreck of *La Belle*. The film includes the dive in 1995 to locate the anomaly, the first cannon recovered, construction of cofferdam, excavation techniques, discovery of a skeleton, dismantling of hull, and conservation of artifacts.

The Shipwreck of La Belle
A film by Alan Govenar

Produced by Documentary Arts in association with La Sept ARTE
Directed by Alan Govenar
Cinematography by Robert Tullier
www.docarts.com

© 1998 Texas Historical Commission

Learning Objectives

Students will learn
1) How the shipwreck of *La Belle* was found
2) What special arrangements were made for the dry land excavation
3) How artifacts were recorded and conserved

Preview

Post these questions for students to consider.
1) How was the shipwreck found?
2) What special arrangements were made for the excavation?
3) How were artifacts recorded?
4) What were the most interesting artifacts?
5) What do the artifacts tell us about the explorers and colonists?

Synopsis (chapters noted)

Note to teachers: you may start and stop the DVD to play the chapters of importance for your lesson.

CHAPTER 1.
Divers from the Texas Historical Commission (THC) discovered a cannon in Matagorda Bay, Texas, in 1995. Archeologist reports to crewmates, "I think we've got a cannon." The cannon was carefully lifted onto a barge. Research was carried out for years in the archives prior to this discovery. When funds were available, special underwater surveying equipment (a magnetometer) was used.

CHAPTER 2.

The cannon had special clues to the identity of the shipwreck: French decorations, crest of Louis XIV, and insignia of Le Comte de Vermandois. The numeral on the brass cannon identified it as one cast in France in 1679.

La Salle was born in Rouen, France, and went to Canada when he was twenty-three. He was first known as a fur trader then as an explorer. His first voyage to the New World was one of discovery and exploration; his second was for settlement.

The expedition left La Rochelle (July 24, 1684) with four ships: *St. Francois* was captured in the Atlantic (1684), *L'Amiable* sank in Pass Cavallo (1685), *Le Joly* returned to France (1685), and *La Belle* sank in Matagorda Bay (1686).

Fort St. Louis was built thirty miles inland. After *La Belle* sank, La Salle journeyed overland to find the Mississippi River, but was assassinated in East Texas in 1687.

CHAPTER 3.

In 1687, the Spanish mapped the shipwreck, then it was forgotten. In 1995, the discovery by THC led to the excavation of *La Belle*. Buoys marked the location of elements of the ship that were still in the sand.

The question was how it should be excavated: with underwater techniques or as a land excavation? Since visibility was zero and *La Belle* was so historically significant, THC decided to conduct a detailed dry land excavation. This required a cofferdam.

The cofferdam was built of pilings

(60 feet long) that were interlocked and driven 41 feet into the sand. Two concentric circles of pilings were set with sand poured in between for a donut effect.

CHAPTER 4.

This cofferdam permitted a detailed excavation from which everything could be recovered. Finds included lead shot, rings, bones of animals, pins, and beads. Everything was recorded with an electronic data system that automatically recorded three coordinates: X, Y, and Z. The outer wall of the cofferdam was 148 feet by 110 feet; the inner opening was 80 feet by 52 feet. When the seawater was drained, artifacts were exposed on the sand but kept moist to prevent shrinkage.

As archeologists worked, the hull of the ship appeared. A swivel gun and a cannon carriage were removed.

Many objects were preserved underwater because the anaerobic environment was oxygen-free and materials did not decay. Early finds included rope, a shoe last, and a skeleton.

CHAPTER 5.

Finding the human skeleton made the whole recovery very personal. The skull was recorded with digital imaging (CT scan). From the scan, a resin model of the skull was created on which to build a facial reconstruction. A forensic anthropologist completed a facial reconstruction by modeling a clay face on the resin skull. From the skull, archeologists could tell that the shipmate had a broken nose and a partially healed

blow to the right side of his head. He had an abscessed tooth that would have been very painful. From the skeleton archeologists could tell that the sailor was male, robust, 5'4" and between 35–45 years old. Brain matter was removed from the skull for DNA that might be matched to descendants. *Content advisory: Dr. Donny Hamilton, a professor at Texas A&M University, discusses a human skull being opened and brain matter being removed. A forensic anthropologist also suggests that bone fragments show scars from syphilis.*

CHAPTER 6.

Excavation of the ship's cargo revealed a crate of muskets known as flintlock guns. Lead munitions survived, but iron rusted in the salt water. The void can be cast to produce the artifact that rusted. Epoxy molding provides a lot of detail.

One box was jacketed in plaster in the excavation and returned to the lab for further investigation. It was wrapped in burlap to move. When the lid was lifted, the archeologists saw rings, brass pins, combs, and mirrors. In La Salle's time, one brass ring would trade for an animal hide.

Other artifacts included a set of brass pots, ladle, and candlesticks: likely the personal possessions of an officer.

CHAPTER 7.

Another crate contained some unique ceramic pots that were recognized as firepots with a wick, flammable material, and a grenade that exploded.

The hull contained many barrels

that were packed densely to stabilize the ship. The final cargo that was uncovered in 1997 included two bronze cannons that matched the first cannon that was found in 1995. A desalinization process, followed by electrolysis, conserved these cannons.

The screening process continued throughout the entire excavation. At the screens small artifacts were found: hawk bells (for trading) and brass dividers (navigational tool). Then the timbers of the ship were traced on plastic and removed. Archeologists decided to dismantle the hull rather than risk breaking it while attempting to move it in one piece. Hundreds of timbers were removed, submerged in seawater and taken to the Texas A&M University Conservation Research Laboratory, where it will take 6–8 years to stabilize the reconstructed hull.

Finally, the sand under the hull was excavated and screened. Then the equipment was removed and the cofferdam dismantled.

CHAPTER 8.

It was a unique project. Over one million artifacts were recovered.

As archeologists study the artifacts they will better understand La Salle and the expedition. The sunken ship contained the necessities of life. The contents of *La Belle* show that the French were geared for success. It was a voyage to establish a permanent settlement in the Mississippi River valley. According to Curtis Tunnel, "if La Salle had succeeded, a lot of North America might be speaking French to this day."

Background

In 1995 archeologists from the Texas Historical Commission located the remains of *La Belle*, the ship that La Salle lost in a storm in 1686. The logistics of an excavation in Matagorda Bay were complex. The decision was made to build a cofferdam in which to conduct a dry land excavation. This excavation in 1996–97 uncovered many artifacts and the hull of the ship. The artifacts and timbers were taken to Texas A&M University Conservation Research Laboratory for conservation.

VOCABULARY

anaerobic: an environment without oxygen; organic materials do not decay in this environment
anomaly: something abnormal or irregular
archeology (archaeology): the study of past cultures through their physical remains
archives: documents preserved for their historical value
artifact: human-made object
buoy: a float
casabelle: knob end of cannon
cofferdam: watertight enclosure built in water, pumped dry to allow work inside
desalinization: remove salt
draft: depth a loaded ship sinks in water
electrolysis: the decomposition of a chemical compound by an electric current
fire pot: ceramic pot used as a weapon in sea warfare
forensic anthropologist: one who

applies crime scene technology to human remains
hawk bell: bells used in falconry to locate a bird, used for trade to Native Americans
musket: type of gun (also called flintlock) that was used in the 1600s
pilings: large supporting timbers, set in the ground
screen: sieve to separate the artifacts from the sand
shoe last: metal mold used in shaping leather into shoes
sump pump: pump used to remove water from a pit

Archeologists in Order of Appearance

Chuck Meide: archeologist/diver who found the first cannon in 1995
Barto Arnold: archeologist who explains procedure for lifting cannon
Curtis Tunnel: executive director of the Texas Historical Commission (THC)
Joe Cozzi: archeologist in the water
Toni Carrell: archeologist on board, assistant project director
Jim Bruseth: project director for THC
Donny Hamilton: Texas A&M University (TAMU) Conservation Research Laboratory
Gentry Steele: TAMU physical anthropologist
Marc McAllister: processed CT information
Reed Williams: explained creation of resin skull
Greg Cook: archeologist who excavated muskets (flint lock guns)

James Jobling: TAMU Conservation
    Research Laboratory
Layne Hedrick: assistant projector
    director
Fred Hocker: TAMU professor

Post View Discussion

Review the posted questions to hear
what the students learned, then pose
this question: Were the artifacts
found in *La Belle* to set up a military
fort or to set up a colony?

Extension

The artifacts from *La Belle* are on
    display in numerous museums
    along the Gulf coast. You may
    read about the exhibits online or
    visit them to see the objects first
    hand.
Seven museums are part of the La
    Salle Odyssey:
Corpus Christi Musuem of Science
    and History (Corpus Christi)
    www.ccmuseum.com
Texas Maritime Museum (Rockport)
    www.texasmaritimemuseum.org
Texana Museum (Edna)
Calhoun County Museum (Port
    Lavaca) www.calhouncountymu
    seum.org
Museum of the Coastal Bend (Victo-
    ria) www.museumofthecoastal
    bend.org
Matagorda County Museum (Bay
    City) www.matagordacountymu
    seum.org
La Petite Belle Homeport (Palacios)
    www.palaciosmuseum.org

Many artifacts are also on display at
    the Texas State History Museum in
    Austin www.thestoryoftexas.com

Dreams of Conquest is a fast-paced visual portrayal of the life of La Salle and archeological investigations of Fort St. Louis. Scenes include the Texas coast, Garcitas Creek, archeological work at Fort St. Louis and Presidio La Bahia and locations in France. It has an excellent audio track and period music.

Dreams of Conquest
A film by Alan Govenar

Produced by Documentary Arts
Directed by Alan Govenar
Cinematography by Robert Tullier
www.docarts.com

© 2004 Texas Historical Commission

Learning Objectives

Students will learn about
1) the early life of La Salle
2) the conflict between France and Spain
3) the French colony in Texas at Fort St. Louis
4) archeological investigations on Garcitas Creek
5) Spanish discoveries of the French fort
6) the Spanish construction of the Presidio La Bahia and accompanying mission
7) how historians and archeologists work

Preview

Post these questions to be answered at the conclusion of the viewing.

1) Why did the French come into the Gulf of Mexico/Mississippi River to set up a colony?
2) Describe the French outpost: Fort St. Louis on Garcitas Creek built by the French in 1685.
3) Do you think that La Salle was a strong leader? Why, or why not?
4) How did the Spanish react to the French intrusion into their territory?
5) Describe Presidio La Bahia, built by the Spanish in 1721.
6) How do archeologists work?

Synopsis (chapters noted)

Note to teachers: you may start and stop the DVD to play the chapters of importance for your lesson.

CHAPTER 1.

This story is inspired by struggle between two world powers (France and Spain) in the seventeenth century and how their conflict affected America.

CHAPTER 2.

Robert Cavalier de la Salle was baptized in 1643 in Rouen, France. He spent his early years in school and as a Catholic priest. His interest in the New World aided France in its challenge to Spain.

CHAPTER 3.

La Salle made two voyages to the New World: first to Canada as an explorer of the Great Lakes and the Mississippi River and second as leader of a colony that crossed the Atlantic Ocean and Gulf of Mexico to Texas. Discovery of cannon on Garcitas Creek in 1996 led to an archeological investigation by Texas Historical Commission.

CHAPTER 4.

The Spanish found Fort St. Louis after the 1689 massacre of the French colonists by the Karankawa tribe. De Leon buried the cannon and several bodies, then mapped and described the settlement. His description matches that of Henri Joutel, chronicler for the expedition.

CHAPTER 5.

Archeologists uncovered a distinct pattern in the soil that showed the outline of the French settlement. An animated portrayal of the settlement matches the magnetometer results to the description. Next the

Spanish fort—Presidio La Bahia—evolves from the magnetometer results.

CHAPTER 6.

The Spanish returned to the site on Garcitas Creek in 1721 to build a presidio and mission across the creek. The outline of excavated buildings and stockade (eight-pointed star) match plans found in the Spanish archives.

CHAPTER 7.

An archeological trench reveals a wall with plaster and allows the stockade to be traced out on the ground. With dedicated work in the field and at the screens, archeologists find ceramics, rings, and shot. While they searched for a French cemetery, it was not located in the 25-acre survey.

CHAPTER 8.

Some animal bones are found. Then human bones are found: the three colonists that de Leon buried (one adult male, one adult female, and one 8-year-old child). Juan Chapa, Spanish soldier with de Leon, wrote a poem to the French woman whom they buried.

CHAPTER 9.

The Karankawa Indians massacred the colonists but spared several children. The children were adopted by the Karankawa and treated very kindly.

CHAPTER 10.

Forensic study of the French skeletons show that cause of death was likely from blow to the head.

CHAPTER 11.

Tension between the French and the Karankawa was caused when La Salle's men took canoes without trading.

CHAPTER 12.

Archeologists consulted historians in France.

CHAPTER 13.

La Salle's life showed personality problems.

CHAPTER 14.

La Salle was difficult to work with. He had some loyal friends but many detractors, especially Minet, who was on the early voyage but sent home on the *Joly*.

CHAPTER 15.

The idea of La Salle's homosexuality is explored (one minute). La Salle made poor choices in selecting the crew and colonists. *Content advisory: A French historian suggests that La Salle may have been homosexual. He also suggests that some of La Salle's actions show poor choices in selecting the crew and colonists to go on the voyage.*

CHAPTER 16.

Supplies were gathered from France for the expedition. Ceramics showed evidence of French at the Garcitas Creek site. The importance of pottery to archeologists is emphasized.

CHAPTER 17.

Connections are made with Rochefort (supply depot established by Colbert) and La Rochelle (the port from which La Salle sailed). A comparison is made between France keeping a colony supplied from Europe and Spain doing so from centers in Mexico. This difference shows up at site of Fort St. Louis and La Bahia.

CHAPTER 18.
Spain was strong in Texas and northern Mexico.

CHAPTER 19.
Trade was of interest to France.

CHAPTER 20.
At Cholula, Mexico, the Spanish built a cathedral on top of the ancient pyramid-temple. Spain controlled the mines and trade of the region.

CHAPTER 21.
When La Salle realized he had only one way to return to France, he made plans to walk to New France (Canada). His men were discouraged and quarreling. They murdered La Salle in East Texas.

CHAPTER 22.
Fort St. Louis collapsed once La Salle and the able-bodied men had gone. Karankawa Indians attacked and massacred most of the remaining colonists. When the Spanish found the settlement in 1690, they burned it to the ground. Later, in 1721, the Spanish returned to the location and built a presidio with a palisade.

CHAPTER 23.
Research shows that Garcitas Creek was only intended to be a temporary location for the French. The goal was still to build on the Mississippi River, in order to control more territory.

CHAPTER 24.
The cemetery for the colony was never located. Its location remains a mystery.

CHAPTER 25.
Only archeological fragments remain to tell the story of the explorers who tried to create a new life in the New World.

Background

After the discovery of a cannon from *La Belle* in 1995 in Matagorda Bay, archeologists excavated the shipwreck in 1996–97. Their investigations triggered additional research into the life and times of La Salle, leader of the ill-fated expedition that landed in Matagorda Bay.

In 1997, eight iron cannons were discovered on property adjacent to Garcitas Creek in Victoria County, Texas. This discovery confirmed the location of Fort St. Louis, occupied by the French for several years. An investigation of that area revealed the later Spanish Presidio La Bahia, built on top of the earlier French settlement from the time of La Salle.

La Salle's story is related in detail as archeologists and historians seek to explain the motivation of La Salle and his impact on the exploration and colonization of the New World.

VOCABULARY

archeology (archaeology): the study of past cultures through their physical remains

artillery: heavy, mounted firearms; cannon

ceramics: clay or porcelain objects

jacal: shelter built with posts and mud

Karankawa: Native Americans along the Gulf coast

kiln: an oven for drying or baking bricks or pottery

league: a measure of distance; about 3 miles

magnetometer: instrument used for measuring the presence of metal

majolica: decorative enameled pottery, first made in Spain, later in Mexico

mission: an organization sent for the spread of religion

sherds: broken pieces of ceramic pottery

presidio: the fort, often near a mission, to protect a settlement

screening: sieving dirt through screen wire to separate artifacts from the soil

People from 1600–1700s

Alonzo de Leon: leader of Spanish expedition that found Fort St. Louis in 1689.

Henri Joutel: Frenchman who kept a journal of the La Salle expedition and returned to France, where he published it as a book

Juan Chapa: Spaniard who drew a map of Fort St. Louis

Jean Baptiste Talon: French boy who was taken by La Salle to live with the Caddo; later returned to France

Jean Baptiste Minet: French navigator who returned to France in 1685

HISTORIANS AND ARCHEOLO-
GISTS in order of appearance:
Curtis Tunnell: executive director of
the Texas Historical Commission
Lynn Edwards: historian
Jim Bruseth: principal inviestigator
for *La Belle* and Fort St. Louis ar-
cheological projects, Archeology
Division Director, Texas Histori-
cal Commission
Mike Davis: archeologist with the
Texas Historical Commission
Robert A. Ricklis: archeologist and
author of *Karankawa Indians*
H. Gill King: historian
Kathleen Gilmore: archeologist with
a specialty in Spanish colonial
history; first identified the French
pottery from the Fort St. Louis
site
Raymonde Litalien: French historian
John De Bry: naval historian
Nicolas Faucherre: French historian

Post View Discussion/Activity

Using the questions posted as preview, encourage students to express
their ideas about La Salle, Fort St.
Louis, and Presidio La Bahia.

1) Why did the French come into the
Gulf of Mexico/Mississippi River
to set up a colony?
2) Describe the French outpost: Fort
St. Louis on Garcitas Creek in 1685.
3) Do you think that La Salle was a
strong leader? Why, or why not?
4) How did the Spanish react to the
French intrusion into their territory?
5) Describe Presidio La Bahia built
by the Spanish in 1721.
6) How do archeologists work?

Extend

Dreams of Conquest shows many
facets of the historical investigations
triggered by the discoveries on the
Texas coast. Ask students what documents they recall and the historical
locations visited.

Making it Relevant

The clue for the location of Fort St.
Louis came from a ranch foreman
who found the cannon in 1996. His
interest in history led him to report
it to the Texas Historical Commission (THC). Since the discovery was
on private property, the THC had to
gain permission from the landown-
ers to do the archeological work.

If you found a buried cannon or
other old weapon, what would you do?

Do you think there are other artifacts that can tell us more about
historical events?

Do you know of any historical
mysteries that remain unsolved?

Unit One — Learning about the Past from a Shipwreck

FOURTH GRADE

4.1 (A) The student will identify Native American groups in Texas and the Western Hemisphere before European exploration and describe the regions in which they lived.

4.2 History. The student understands the causes and effects of European exploration and colonization of Texas and the Western Hemisphere.

(A) The student will summarize reasons for European exploration and settlement of Texas and the Western Hemisphere.

(B) The student will identify the accomplishments of significant explorers and explain their impact on the settlement of Texas.

4.6 Geography. The student uses geographic tools to collect, analyze and interpret data.

4.8 Geography. The student understands the location and patterns of settlement and the geographic factors that influence where people live.

4.9 Geography. The student understands how people adapt to and modify their environment.

4.10 Economics. The student understands the basic economic patterns of early societies in Texas and the Western Hemisphere.

4.11 Economics. The student understands the reasons for exploration and colonization.

4.20 Culture. The student understands the contributions of people of various racial, ethnic, and religious groups to Texas.

4.22 Social studies skills. The student applies critical-thinking skills to organize and use information acquired from a variety of sources, including electronic technology.

4.23 Social studies skills. The student communicates in written, oral, and visual forms.

4.24 Social studies skills. The student uses problem-solving and decision-making skills, working independently and with others in a variety of settings.

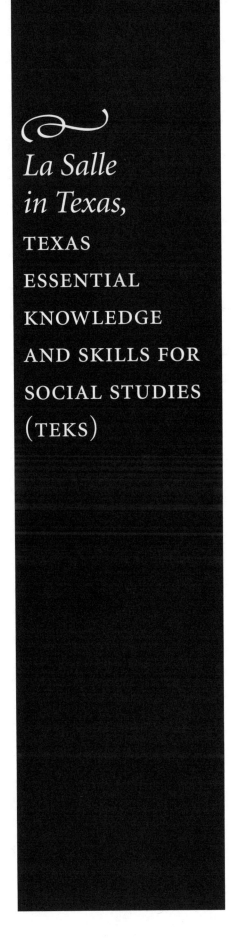

La Salle in Texas, TEXAS ESSENTIAL KNOWLEDGE AND SKILLS FOR SOCIAL STUDIES (TEKS)

FIFTH GRADE

5.1 History. The student understands the causes and effects of European colonization in the United States.
(A) The student is expected to explain when, where, and why groups of people colonized and settled in the United States.

5.6 Geography. The student uses geographic tools to collect, analyze, and interpret data.
5.9 Geography. The student understands how people adapt to and modify their environment.

5.10 Economics. The student understands the basic economic patterns of early societies in the United States.
(A) The student is expected to explain the economic patterns of various early Native American groups in the United States.
5.11 Economics. The student understands the reasons for exploration and colonization.
(A) The student is expected to identify the economic motivation for European exploration and settlement in the United States.

5.25 Social studies skills. The student applies critical thinking skills to organize and use information acquired from a variety of sources, including electronic technology.
5.26 Social studies skill. The student communicates in written, oral, and visual forms.
5.27 Social studies skills. The student uses problem-solving and decision making skills, working

independently and with others in a variety of settings.

SIXTH GRADE

6.2 History. The student understands the contributions of individuals and groups from various cultures to selected historical and contemporary societies.

6.3 Geography. The student uses maps, globes, graphs, charts, models, and databases to answer geographic questions.
6.7 Geography. The student understands the impact of interactions between people and the physical environment on the development of places and regions.
(A) The student is expected to identify and analyze ways people have adapted to the physical environment in selected places and regions.

6.8 Economics. The student understands the various ways in which people organize economic systems.
(A) The student is expected to compare ways in which various societies organize the production and distribution of goods and services.

6.14 Citizenship. The student understands the relationship among individual rights, responsibilities, and freedoms in democratic societies.

6.15 Culture. The student understands the similarities and differ-

ences within and among cultures in different societies.
6.16 Culture. The student understands that certain institutions are basic to all societies but characteristics of these institutions may vary from one society to another.

6.21 Social studies skills. The student applies critical thinking skills to organize and use information acquired from a variety of sources, including electronic technology.
6.22 Social studies skills. The student communicates in written, oral, and visual forms.
6.23 Social studies skills. The student uses problem-solving and decision making skills, working independently and with others in a variety of settings.

SEVENTH GRADE

7.1 History. The student understands traditional historical points of reference in Texas history.
(A) The student will identify the major eras in Texas history and describe their defining characteristics;
(B) The student will apply absolute and relative chronology through the sequencing of significant individuals, events, and time periods;
7.2 History. The student understands how individuals, events, and issues prior to the Texas Revolution shaped the history of Texas.
(B) The student will identify important individuals, events, and issues related to European exploration and colonization of Texas.

7.9 Geography. The student understands the location and characteristics of places and regions of Texas.

(C) The student will analyze the effects of physical and human factors such as climate, weather, landforms, irrigation, transportation, and communication on major events in Texas.

7.16 Citizenship. The student understands the rights and responsibilities of Texas citizens.

7.21 Social Studies Skills. The student applies critical thinking skills to organize and use information acquired from a variety of sources, including electronic technology.

7.22 Social Studies Skills. The student communicates in written, oral, and visual forms.

7.23 Social Studies Skills. The student uses problem-solving and decision-making skills, working independently and with others in a variety of settings.

EIGHTH GRADE

8.1 History. The student understands traditional historical points of reference in U.S. history through 1877.

8.2 History. The student understands the causes of exploration and colonization eras.

8.10 Geography. The student uses geographic tools to collect, analyze, and interpret data.

8.11 Geography. The student understands the location and character-

istics of places and regions of the United States, past and present.

8.20 Citizenship. The student understands the rights and responsibilities of citizens of the United States.

8.24 Culture. The student understands the relationship between and among people from various groups, including racial, ethnic, and religious groups, during the 17th, 18th, and 19th centuries.

8.30 Social Studies Skills. The student applies critical thinking skills to organize and use information acquired from a variety of sources, including electronic technology.

8.31 Social Studies Skills. The student communicates in written, oral, and visual forms.

8.32 Social Studies Skills. The student uses problem-solving and decision-making skills, working independently and with others in a variety of settings.

Unit Two — Be an Archeologist

FOURTH GRADE

1.2 (A) The student will identify Native American groups in Texas and the Western Hemisphere before European exploration and describe the regions in which they lived.

4.2 History. The student understands the causes and effects of European exploration and colo-

nization of Texas and the Western Hemisphere.

(C) The student will summarize reasons for European exploration and settlement of Texas and the Western Hemisphere.

(D) The student will identify the accomplishments of significant explorers and explain their impact on the settlement of Texas.

4.6 Geography. The student uses geographic tools to collect, analyze, and interpret data.

4.8 Geography. The student understands the location and patterns of settlement and the geographic factors that influence where people live.

4.9 Geography. The student understands how people adapt to and modify their environment.

4.10 Economics. The student understands the basic economic patterns of early societies in Texas and the Western Hemisphere.

4.11 Economics. The student understands the reasons for exploration and colonization.

4.22 Social studies skills. The student applies critical-thinking skills to organize and use information acquired from a variety of sources, including electronic technology.

4.23 Social studies skills. The student communicates in written, oral, and visual forms.

4.24 Social studies skills. The student uses problem-solving and decision-making skills, working independently and with others in a variety of settings.

FIFTH GRADE

5.1 History. The student understands the causes and effects of European colonization in the United States.

5.6 Geography. The student uses geographic tools to collect, analyze, and interpret data.

5.9 Geography. The student understands how people adapt to and modify their environment.

5.10 Economics. The student understands the basic economic patterns of early societies in the United States.

(A) The student is expected to explain the economic patterns of various early Native American groups in the United States.

5.11 Economics. The student understands the reasons for exploration and colonization.

(A) The student is expected to identify the economic motivation for European exploration and settlement in the United States.

5.25 Social studies skills. The student applies critical thinking skills to organize and use information acquired from a variety of sources, including electronic technology.

5.26 Social studies skill. The student communicates in written, oral, and visual forms.

5.27 Social studies skills. The student uses problem-solving and decision making skills, working independently and with others in a variety of settings.

SIXTH GRADE

6.2 History. The student understands the contributions of individuals and groups from various cultures to selected historical and contemporary societies.

6.3 Geography. The student uses maps, globes, graphs, charts, models, and databases to answer geographic questions.

6.7 Geography. The student understands the impact of interactions between people and the physical environment on the development of places and regions.

(A) The student is expected to identify and analyze ways people have adapted to the physical environment in selected places and regions.

6.8 Economics. The student understands the various ways in which people organize economic systems.

(A) The student is expected to compare ways in which various societies organize the production and distribution of goods and services.

6.14 Citizenship. The student understands the relationship among individual rights, responsibilities, and freedoms in democratic societies.

6.21 Social studies skills. The student applies critical thinking skills to organize and use information acquired from a variety of sources, including electronic technology.

6.22 Social studies skills. The student communicates in written, oral, and visual forms.

6.23 Social studies skills. The student uses problem-solving and decision making skills, working independently and with others in a variety of settings.

SEVENTH GRADE

7.1 History. The student understands traditional historical points of reference in Texas history.

7.2 History. The student understands how individuals, events, and issues prior to the Texas Revolution shaped the history of Texas.

(C) The student will identify important individuals, events, and issues related to European exploration and colonization of Texas.

7.9 Geography. The student understands the location and characteristics of places and regions of Texas.

7.16 Citizenship. The student understands the rights and responsibilities of Texas citizens.

7.23 Social Studies Skills. The student applies critical thinking skills to organize and use information acquired from a variety of sources, including electronic technology.

7.24 Social Studies Skills. The student communicates in written, oral, and visual forms.

7.23 Social Studies Skills. The student uses problem-solving and decision-making skills, working independently and with others in a variety of settings.

EIGHTH GRADE

8.1 History. The student understands traditional historical points of reference in U.S. history through 1877.

8.2 History. The student understands the causes of exploration and colonization eras.

8.10 Geography. The student uses geographic tools to collect, analyze, and interpret data.

8.11 Geography. The student understands the location and characteristics of places and regions of the United States, past and present.

8.20 Citizenship. The student understands the rights and responsibilities of citizens of the United States.

8.24 Culture. The student understands the relationship between and among people from various groups, including racial, ethnic, and religious groups, during the 17th, 18th, and 19th centuries.

8.30 Social Studies Skills. The student applies critical thinking skills to organize and use information acquired from a variety of sources, including electronic technology.

8.31 Social Studies Skills. The student communicates in written, oral, and visual forms.

8.32 Social Studies Skills. The student uses problem-solving and decision-making skills, working independently and with others in a variety of settings.

Unit Three — Journeys in the New World

FOURTH GRADE

4.3 (A) The student will identify Native American groups in Texas and the Western Hemisphere before European exploration and describe the regions in which they lived.

4.2 History. The student understands the causes and effects of European exploration and colonization of Texas and the Western Hemisphere.

(E) The student will summarize reasons for European exploration and settlement of Texas and the Western Hemisphere.

(F) The student will identify the accomplishments of significant explorers and explain their impact on the settlement of Texas.

4.6 Geography. The student uses geographic tools to collect, analyze, and interpret data.

4.8 Geography. The student understands the location and patterns of settlement and the geographic factors that influence where people live.

4.9 Geography. The student understands how people adapt to and modify their environment.

4.10 Economics. The student understands the basic economic patterns of early societies in Texas and the Western Hemisphere.

4.11 Economics. The student understands the reasons for exploration and colonization.

4.20 Culture. The student understands the contributions of people of various racial, ethnic, and religious groups to Texas.

4.22 Social studies skills. The student applies critical-thinking skills to organize and use information acquired from a variety of sources, including electronic technology.

4.23 Social studies skills. The student communicates in written, oral, and visual forms.

4.24 Social studies skills. The student uses problem-solving and decision-making skills, working independently and with others in a variety of settings.

FIFTH GRADE

5.1 History. The student understands the causes and effects of European colonization in the United States.

(A) The student is expected to explain when, where, and why groups of people colonized and settled in the United States.

5.6 Geography. The student uses geographic tools to collect, analyze, and interpret data.

5.9 Geography. The student understands how people adapt to and modify their environment.

5.10 Economics. The student understands the basic economic patterns of early societies in the United States.

(A) The student is expected to explain the economic patterns of various early Native American groups in the United States.

5.11 Economics. The student understands the reasons for exploration and colonization.
(A) The student is expected to identify the economic motivation for European exploration and settlement in the United States.

5.25 Social studies skills. The student applies critical thinking skills to organize and use information acquired from a variety of sources, including electronic technology.
5.26 Social studies skills. The student communicates in written, oral, and visual forms.
5.27 Social studies skills. The student uses problem-solving and decision-making skills, working independently and with others in a variety of settings.

SIXTH GRADE

6.2 History. The student understands the contributions of individuals and groups from various cultures to selected historical and contemporary societies.

6.3 Geography. The student uses maps, globes, graphs, charts, models, and databases to answer geographic questions.
6.7 Geography. The student understands the impact of interactions between people and the physical environment on the development of places and regions.
(A) The student is expected to identify and analyze ways people have adapted to the physical environment in selected places and regions.

6.8 Economics. The student understands the various ways in which people organize economic systems.
(A) The student is expected to compare ways in which various societies organize the production and distribution of goods and services.

6.14 Citizenship. The student understands the relationship among individual rights, responsibilities, and freedoms in democratic societies.

6.15 Culture. The student understands the similarities and differences within and among cultures in different societies.
6.16 Culture. The student understands that certain institutions are basic to all societies, but characteristics of these institutions may vary from one society to another.

6.21 Social studies skills. The student applies critical thinking skills to organize and use information acquired from a variety of sources, including electronic technology.
6.22 Social studies skills. The student communicates in written, oral, and visual forms.
6.23 Social studies skills. The student uses problem-solving and decision-making skills, working independently and with others in a variety of settings.

SEVENTH GRADE

7.1 History. The student understands traditional historical points of reference in Texas history.

(C) The student will identify the major eras in Texas history and describe their defining characteristics.
(D) The student will apply absolute and relative chronology through the sequencing of significant individuals, events, and time periods.
7.2 History. The student understands how individuals, events, and issues prior to the Texas Revolution shaped the history of Texas.
(D) The student will identify important individuals, events, and issues related to European exploration and colonization of Texas.

7.11 Geography. The student understands the location and characteristics of places and regions of Texas.
(C) The student will analyze the effects of physical and human factors such as climate, weather, landforms, irrigation, transportation, and communication on major events in Texas.

7.16 Citizenship. The student understands the rights and responsibilities of Texas citizens.

7.25 Social Studies Skills. The student applies critical thinking skills to organize and use information acquired from a variety of sources, including electronic technology.
7.26 Social Studies Skills. The student communicates in written, oral, and visual forms.
7.23 Social Studies Skills. The student uses problem-solving and decision-making skills, working independently and with others in a variety of settings.

EIGHTH GRADE

8.1 History. The student understands traditional historical points of reference in U.S. history through 1877.

8.2 History. The student understands the causes of exploration and colonization eras.

8.10 Geography. The student uses geographic tools to collect, analyze, and interpret data.

8.11 Geography. The student understands the location and characteristics of places and regions of the United States, past and present.

8.20 Citizenship. The student understands the rights and responsibilities of citizens of the United States.

8.24 Culture. The student understands the relationship between and among people from various groups, including racial, ethnic, and religious groups during the 17th, 18th, and 19th centuries.

8.30 Social Studies Skills. The student applies critical thinking skills to organize and use information acquired from a variety of sources, including electronic technology.

8.31 Social Studies Skills. The student communicates in written, oral, and visual forms.

8.32 Social Studies Skills. The student uses problem-solving and decision-making skills, working independently and with others in a variety of settings.

Unit Four — Surviving Along the Gulf Coast

FOURTH GRADE

4.4 (A) The student will identify Native American groups in Texas and the Western Hemisphere before European exploration and describe the regions in which they lived.

4.2 History. The student understands the causes and effects of European exploration and colonization of Texas and the Western Hemisphere.

(G) The student will summarize reasons for European exploration and settlement of Texas and the Western Hemisphere.

(H) The student will identify the accomplishments of significant explorers and explain their impact on the settlement of Texas.

4.6 Geography. The student uses geographic tools to collect, analyze, and interpret data.

4.8 Geography. The student understands the location and patterns of settlement and the geographic factors that influence where people live.

4.9 Geography. The student understands how people adapt to and modify their environment.

4.10 Economics. The student understands the basic economic patterns of early societies in Texas and the Western Hemisphere.

4.11 Economics. The student understands the reasons for exploration and colonization.

4.20 Culture. The student understands the contributions of people of various racial, ethnic, and religious groups to Texas.

4.22 Social studies skills. The student applies critical-thinking skills to organize and use information acquired from a variety of sources, including electronic technology.

4.23 Social studies skills. The student communicates in written, oral, and visual forms.

4.24 Social studies skills. The student uses problem-solving and decision-making skills, working independently and with others in a variety of settings.

FIFTH GRADE

5.1 History. The student understands the causes and effects of European colonization in the United States.

(A) The students is expected to explain when, where, and why groups of people colonized and settled in the United States.

5.6 Geography. The student uses geographic tools to collect, analyze, and interpret data.

5.9 Geography. The student understands how people adapt to and modify their environment.

5.10 Economics. The student understands the basic economic patterns of early societies in the United States.

(A) The student is expected to explain the economic patterns of various early Native American groups in the United States.

5.11 Economics. The student understands the reasons for exploration and colonization.
(A) The student is expected to identify the economic motivation for European exploration and settlement in the United States.

5.25 Social studies skills. The student applies critical thinking skills to organize and use information acquired from a variety of sources, including electronic technology.
5.26 Social studies skill. The student communicates in written, oral, and visual forms.
5.27 Social studies skills. The student uses problem-solving and decision-making skills, working independently and with others in a variety of settings.

SIXTH GRADE

6.2 History. The student understands the contributions of individuals and groups from various cultures to selected historical and contemporary societies.

6.3 Geography. The student uses maps, globes, graphs, charts, models, and databases to answer geographic questions.
6.7 Geography. The student understands the impact of interactions between people and the physical environment on the development of places and regions.
(A) The student is expected to identify and analyze ways people have adapted to the physical environment in selected places and regions.

6.8 Economics. The student understands the various ways in which people organize economic systems.
(A) The student is expected to compare ways in which various societies organize the production and distribution of goods and services.

6.14 Citizenship. The student understands the relationship among individual rights, responsibilities, and freedoms in democratic societies.

6.15 Culture. The student understands the similarities and differences within and among cultures in different societies.
6.16 Culture. The student understands that certain institutions are basic to all societies, but characteristics of these institutions may vary from one society to another.

6.21 Social studies skills. The student applies critical thinking skills to organize and use information acquired from a variety of sources, including electronic technology.
6.22 Social studies skills. The student communicates in written, oral, and visual forms.
6.23 Social studies skills. The student uses problem-solving and decision-making skills, working independently and with others in a variety of settings.

SEVENTH GRADE

7.1 History. The student understands traditional historical points of reference in Texas history.

(E) The student will identify the major eras in Texas history and describe their defining characteristics.
(F) The student will apply absolute and relative chronology through the sequencing of significant individuals, events, and time periods.
7.2 History. The student understands how individuals, events, and issues prior to the Texas Revolution shaped the history of Texas.
(E) The student will identify important individuals, events, and issues related to European exploration and colonization of Texas.

7.12 Geography. The student understands the location and characteristics of places and regions of Texas.
(C) The student will analyze the effects of physical and human factors such as climate, weather, landforms, irrigation, transportation, and communication on major events in Texas.

7.16 Citizenship. The student understands the rights and responsibilities of Texas citizens.

7.27 Social Studies Skills. The student applies critical thinking skills to organize and use information acquired from a variety of sources, including electronic technology.
21.28 Social Studies Skills. The student communicates in written, oral, and visual forms.
7.23 Social Studies Skills. The student uses problem-solving and decision-making skills, working independently and with others in a variety of settings.

EIGHTH GRADE

8.1 History. The student understands traditional historical points of reference in U.S. history through 1877.

8.2 History. The student understands the causes of exploration and colonization eras.

8.10 Geography. The student uses geographic tools to collect, analyze, and interpret data.

8.11 Geography. The student understands the location and characteristics of places and regions of the United States, past and present.

8.20 Citizenship. The student understands the rights and responsibilities of citizens of the United States.

8.24 Culture. The student understands the relationship between and among people from various groups, including racial, ethnic and religious groups, during the 17th, 18th, and 19th centuries.

8.30 Social Studies Skills. The student applies critical thinking skills to organize and use information acquired from a variety of sources, including electronic technology.

8.31 Social Studies Skills. The student communicates in written, oral, and visual forms.

8.32 Social Studies Skills. The student uses problem-solving and decision-making skills, working independently and with others in a variety of settings.

Note that most lesson ideas for Unit Two are incorporated into the unit and are not represented here.

Language Arts

(From Unit One)
1) Write a journal entry as if you were one of the historical characters listed in the assignment.
2) Write and publish a newspaper or web site about the La Salle expedition.

(From Unit Three)
1) Create an advertisement to recruit colonists to sail with La Salle.
2) Write a journal entry as a historical character (La Salle, Joutel, Abbé Cavelier, King Louis XIV) or recall an event or occasion of importance to you and write a journal entry about that.

(From Unit Four)
1) Write a journal as if you were a member of one of the cultures represented. See "The French in Texas" lesson at www.texasbeyondhistory.net/belle/lesson.html
2) Find a record of Native American languages. Create a story using another language.
3) Create a poster or brochure to advertise the La Salle Odyssey trail.

Seven museums are included in the La Salle Odyssey trail:

Corpus Christi Museum of Science and History (Corpus Christi) www.ccmuseum.com

Texas Maritime Museum (Rockport) www.texasmaritimemuseum.org

Texana Museum (Edna) (no web site at time of writing)

Calhoun County Museum (Port Lavaca) www.calhouncountymuseum.org

Museum of the Coastal Bend (Victoria) www.museumofthecoastalbend.org

Matagorda County Museum (Bay City) www.matagordacountymuseum.org

La Petite Belle Homeport (Palacios) www.palaciosmuseum.org

Citizenship—Ethics

(From Unit One)
1) Collectors: These mystery items were found on *La Belle*: Roman coin (*FWG*, p. 110), fica (Spanish charm), (*FWG*, p. 111), fossil (ammonite) (*FWG*, p. 111) arrow point (Cuney type) (*FWG*, p. 111–112)
How did these objects get on the ship? They seem to be out of place

(without context). Were they objects that the sailors and officers collected? What will happen to artifacts that modern collectors leave in a garage or shoe box?

2) Pirates: Pirates were legendary in the seventeenth century. La Salle and his expedition encountered them several times. Do we have "pirates" in the twenty-first century? (Such as people who use public water sources without paying taxes or use fees, people who illegally copy Internet songs and movies)

3) Immigrants: Colonists who came to Texas with La Salle were planning a new life in a foreign country. What parallels do we have today? (graduate foreign students, green card workers, illegal immigrants, other)

4) Who owns sunken ships? There is often debate between salvagers who locate the shipwreck and governments (nation or state) who claim ownership (*FWG* p. 72). See www.pbs.org/wgbh/nova/la salle/

Art/Language Arts/Computer

(from Unit One)

1) Create a brochure or web site advertising the La Salle Odyssey, a trail of museums that displays the story and artifacts from *La Belle* and Fort St. Louis.

Seven museums are part of the La Salle Odyssey:

Corpus Christi Museum of Science and History (Corpus Christi) www.ccmuseum.com

Texas Maritime Museum (Rockport) www.texasmaritimemuseum.org

Texana Museum (Edna) (no web site available at time of writing)

Calhoun County Museum (Port Lavaca) www.calhouncountymu seum.org

Museum of the Coastal Bend (Victoria) www.museumofthecoastal bend.org

Matagorda County Museum (Bay City) www.matagordacountymu seum.org

La Petite Belle Homeport (Palacios) www.palaciosmuseum.org

Math

(from Unit One)

1) Calculate the square foot space on the deck of the ship. Compare to space in classroom or on playground.

2) What does the "draft" of a ship mean? How deep is Matagorda Bay today? Could *La Belle* sail through Pass Cavallo into Matagorda Bay today?

3) Study the geometry of shipbuilding. What does it take to float a boat?

4) Calculate the ocean's pressure and predict its effect on the shipwreck underwater.

(from Unit Three)

1) Calculate the trek from Texas to Canada. The surviving Frenchmen walked from Texas to Canada (approximately 1200 miles) after *La Belle* was wrecked in the storm. Calculate how long it takes for you to walk one (1) mile. If you walked 8 hours a day, how many days would it take you to walk the same distance as the French trek in 1687–88?

2) Problems related to voyages:

a) How many days did it take La Salle to cross the Atlantic Ocean? He left France August 1, 1684 and arrived in Haiti/Santo Domingo September 27, 1684.

b) La Salle set sail from Santo Domingo on November 25, 1684 and arrived on the Gulf Coast January 1, 1685. How many days did he sail?

c) How many total days did he sail from France to the Gulf Coast?

d) Using the number of total days La Salle traveled and assuming that he traveled 5000 miles, how far did he travel each day, on average?

e) If La Salle only sailed 10 hours each day, how fast was the expedition traveling?

f) Today a plane averages 625 miles per hour. How many hours would the same 5000-mile trip take?

(from Unit Four)

1) LaSalle and his men traveled from Fort St. Louis to the Caddo villages (near Nacogdoches) to trade. Determine how many miles that trip would be. _____ (approx. 325 miles). If they walked 15 miles a day, how many days would that trip take? _____ (16).

2) The Jumano were messengers and traders for the Spanish. They traveled from near Presidio to El Paso to tell the Spanish about the French fort on the coast. How far was that journey? _____ (approx. 200 miles). If they traveled 15 miles a day, how long would it take them? _____ (13 days).

Science

(from Unit One)

1) Experiment to see how a ship might sink. See Buoyancy Brainteasers at www.pbs.org/wgbh/nova/lasalle/buoyancy

2) *La Belle* was in an anaerobic environment after it sank. What does this mean? Develop and conduct experiments testing how fast objects decay in various environments.

3) Research and use navigational devices, past and present.

4) What are the ecological impacts of excavation—underwater and on land?

5) Research and analyze the diet of seventeenth-century sailors and colonists. Compare it to your diet.

6) Learn about other famous shipwrecks such as *Mary Rose*, *Vasa*, and *Titanic* and compare their recoveries to that of *La Belle*.

7) Learn more about conservation of artifacts—especially wood and metal—from underwater sites.

(from Unit Three)
Research and use navigational instruments.

Social Studies/Internet

(from Unit One)
Use the La Salle story to participate in National History Day. Theme for 2007: Triumph and Tragedy in History. 2008: The Individual in History. See the web site for National History Day for further information (www.nationalhistoryday.org).

(from Unit Three)
You have been selected to set up a colony—in 1600s on the Gulf coast or today on the moon. Create a plan that would include considerations about location, what to do if inhabited, supplies to pack, what work needs to be done on arrival, and who will go.

Geography

(From Unit Three)

1) Comparing maps. Find a map of the time of La Salle (1692 by Rouillard from Le Cerieq included in the unit) to see how geographic features were shown in 1600s. Overlay a modern map of North America on one of these to see reasons La Salle missed the mouth of the Mississippi River when he sailed along the coast in 1684.

2) What different environments did the expedition pass through?

(from Unit Four)

1) Locate a map that shows Native American tribes today. Which ones do you have in your state?

2) How do the different topographic zones relate to the adaptation by the early cultures?

3) When thinking about how the early people traveled, we need to remember that the rivers (and valleys) were like highways. Compare distance by river and by highway from San Antonio to Seadrift; from Dallas to Anahuac; others.

Visual Arts

(from Unit Three)
Create a board game based on La Salle's journeys; or develop as a computer game.

(from Unit Four)
Find information on the regalia and dances of Native American tribes near you. If possible, visit and participate in a Powwow. Tell your class about your experience.

GLOSSARY

Unit One: Learning about the Past from a Shipwreck

Aft: rear section of a ship

Anaerobic: an environment without oxygen; organic materials do not decay in this environment

Anomaly: something abnormal or irregular

Archeology (archaeology): the study of past cultures through their physical remains

Archives: documents preserved for their historical value

Artifact: an object that has been made or modified by people

Bilge pump: pump used to remove water from lowest compartment of a ship

Bow: front section of the ship

Buoy: a float

Cargo: goods and weapons stored for transport

Casabelle: knob end of cannon

Cask: small barrel for storage

Cofferdam: watertight enclosure built in water, pumped dry to allow work inside

Colony: people who settle in a new country but are subject to the mother country

Desalinization: remove salt

Draft: depth a floating ship sinks in water

Electronic Data Station: surveying instrument that records exact location of objects in a computer to aid in mapping

Electrolysis: the decomposition of a chemical compound by an electric current

Fire pot: ceramic pot used as a weapon in sea warfare

Forensic anthropologist: one who applies crime scene technology to human remains

Hawk bell: bells used in falconry to locate a bird, used for trade to Native Americans

Hull: outer structure of a ship

Lazarette: most aft section of ship, often housed explosives

Magnetometer: instrument for measuring the presence of metal

Musket: type of gun (also called flintlock) that was used in the 1600s

Pilings: large supporting timber, set in the ground

Porringer: dish the size of a cereal bowl

Screen: sieve to separate the artifacts from the sand

Sump pump: pump used to remove water from a pit (in this instance from the cofferdam)

Unit Two: Be an Archeologist

Adzes: chisel-like tool, used as a wedge

Altitude: measure of elevation

Anomaly: something abnormal or irregular

Archeology (archaeology): the study of past cultures through their material remains

Artifact: an object that has been made or modified by people

Astrolabe: an instrument formerly used for taking altitude of the stars at sea, superceded by the quadrant and sextant

Attribute: characteristic that can be assigned

Classify: to arrange in a set or group according to common attributes

Cofferdam: watertight enclosure built in water, pumped dry to allow work inside

Context: surrounding environment, association

Coordinates: a set of numbers that locates a point in space in relation to a system of lines

Data: facts or information

Dilemma: a situation requiring a choice between equally objectionable alternatives

Dividers: instrument used for navigation as compass (protractor)

Ethics: rules of conduct

Falconry: sport in Europe where falcons retrieve game

Firepot: ceramic vessel filled with flammable material and a grenade, something like a Molotov cocktail

Grid: framework of parallel and perpendicular lines

Hawking bell: brass bell attached to a falcon's leg to sound its location

Inference: derived by reasoning; conclusion drawn from evidence

Latitude: distance north or south of the equator

Lazarette: stern hold on a ship

Longitude: distance east or west of prime meridian (Greenwich, England)

Magnetometer: instrument used for measuring the presence of metal

Musket: gun of the 16th and 17th century; ignited by spark on powder created by flint

Observation: taking note; paying attention

Pewter: metal alloy of tin and lead

Pipe: long-stemmed ceramic pipe for smoking tobacco

Plot: to mark on a map

Polaris: a star known as the North Star located at the tip of the handle of the Little Dipper; star at which the earth's axis points

Powder flask: container used to keep powder available for loading into musket

Screen: (n.) a frame containing mesh; (v.) to press soil or shake through a screen and recover artifacts

Shot: iron balls used in cannon and muskets, vary in size

Signet: small seal used to make an impression in wax on documents

Trowel: tool resembling a small, flat spade

Vandalism: willful destruction of property

Unit Three: Journeys in the New World

Archeology (archaeology): the study of past cultures through their material remains

Artillery: heavy, mounted firearms; cannon

Buccaneers: French pirates on the Caribbean islands who were named from the smoked meat they prepared

Ceramics: clay or porcelain objects; pottery

Depot: warehouse or distribution point for supplies

Jacal: shelter built with posts and mud

Jesuit order: branch of the Catholic Church who were active missionaries

Karankawa: Native Americans who lived along the Gulf coast

Kiln: an oven for drying or baking bricks or pottery

League: a measure of distance; about 3 miles

Magnetometer: instrument used for measuring the presence of metal

Majolica: decorative enameled pottery, first made in Spain, then Mexico

Mission: an organization sent for the spread of religion; also the buildings for that purpose

Outpost: combination fort and trading post on the edge of a settlement

Sherd (shard): a piece of broken pottery

Pass: channel between bodies of water

Presidio: the fort, often near a mission, to protect a settlement

Privateers: pirates who often had the blessing and protection of a monarch

Screening: sieving dirt through screen wire to separate artifacts from the soil

Unit Four: Surviving along the Gulf Coast

Adobe: sun-dried mud brick used in construction

Artifacts: any object made or modified by people

Ba-ak: Karankawa word for shelter, a lean-to that housed 7–9 people

Band: group that lives and travels together, usually an extended family of 15–25 people

Caddo: Native Americans who lived in East Texas woodlands

Cannibal: eater of human flesh

Clergy: ministers; men set apart to the service of God in the Christian church

Customs: habits; ways of living

Culture: way of life, patterns for living

Dressed hide: animal skin that has been processed to use

Economy: ways to earn a living; management of resources; means of subsistence

Franciscans: Catholic priests from the order of St. Francis, missionaries to the New World

Friar: man belonging to one of the Roman Catholic orders or brotherhood

Job specialization: people do one craft to earn a living and trade that specialty for other needs; for example, an arrow maker would trade arrows for food or pottery

Jumano: Native Americans who lived in Central West Texas along the Concho River

Karankawa: Native Americans who lived along the Gulf coast

Masonry: stone, brick, or concrete construction

Midden: trash pile

Mission: buildings for the priests (friars) and Indians whom they trained in Christianity

Musket: flintlock gun, weapon of 16th and 17th centuries

Outpost: combination fort and trading post on the edge of settlement

Presidio: the fort, often near a mission, to protect a settlement

Ritual: ceremonies

Subsistence: that which furnishes support for life; to be maintained with food and clothing

BIBLIOGRAPHY

Unit One — LEARNING ABOUT THE PAST FROM A SHIPWRECK

Everett, Felicity and Struan Reid. *The Usborne Book of Explorers.* Tulsa, Okla.: EDC Publishing, 1991. Intermediate/youth. Overview of the explorers and routes traveled. Well-illustrated.

Macaulay, David. *Ship.* Boston: Houghton Mifflin, 1993. Intermediate/youth. Well-illustrated story of ship building in the 1600s. Excellent drawings and diagrams.

Mitchell, Mark G. *Raising* La Belle*: The Story of the La Salle Shipwreck.* Austin: Eakin Press, 2002. Intermediate/youth. An account of the excavation of *La Belle* intertwined with the story of La Salle. Intended for middle school audience.

Weddle, Robert S. *The Wreck of the Belle, the Ruin of La Salle.* College Station, Texas: Texas A&M University Press, 2001. Adult. Historian's account of La Salle's expedition and the consequences of the shipwreck.

Weddle, Robert S. (Editor), *La Salle, the Mississippi, and the Gulf: Three Primary Documents.* College Station, Texas: Texas A&M University Press, 1987. Adult. Primary accounts of the Talon children who were part of the expedition. Also reports by Minet, the pilot on the ocean voyage.

Zronik, John. *Sieur de La Salle: New World Adventurer.* New York: Crabtree Publishing Company, 2006. Intermediate/youth. Colorful, well-illustrated story of La Salle. Good background information.

Unit Two — BE AN ARCHEOLOGIST

Archeology. Boy Scouts of America. Merit Badge Series. Intermediate/youth. Written as a guide for leaders to present archeology. Includes a well-defined overview of archeology, requirements for the merit badge, and sources for information.

Archeology in the Classroom. Austin: Texas Historical Commission, 1997. Adult. Teacher manual on archeology with background information and classroom lessons.

Batten, Mary. *Anthropologists: Scientists of the People.* Boston: Houghton Mifflin, 2001. Intermediate/youth. Written to introduce anthropology as a career

Cole, J. and B. Degen. *Magic School Bus Shows and Tells: A Book about Archeology.* Scholastic, 1997. Elementary/youth. Well-illustrated episode of the Magic School Bus. Clear description of the process of archeology.

Duke, Katie. *Archeologists Dig f or Clues.* New York: Harper Collins Publishers, 1997. Elementary/youth. Well-defined story about the process of archeology.

Greenburg, Lorna. *Digging into the Past: Pioneers of Archeology.* New York: Watts, 2001. Intermediate/youth level. Biographies of early leaders in the field of archeology.

Laubstein, Karen. *Archeology Smart.* New York: Random House, 1997. Intemediate/youth. An interactive story that explains the concepts of archeology in a story form.

Starnes, Gigi. *Grandmother's Tales: Discovering Archeology.* Austin: Eakin Press, 1995. Elementary/youth. A story about several children accompanying their grandmother on a summer dig.

Wheat, Pam. *A Beautiful Historic Discovery.* Cobblestone Magazine. October 1999. Intermediate/youth. Short article about the excavation of *La Belle.* Part of an issue on La Salle.

Unit Three — *JOURNEYS IN THE NEW WORLD*

Donaldson-Forbes, Jeff. *La Salle.* New York: Power Kids Press, 2002. Intermediate/youth. Story of La Salle told for youth. Many illustrations enhance the narrative.

Foster, William C. *Spanish Expeditions Into Texas, 1689–1768.* University of Texas Press, 1995. Adult. Good summary of Spanish in Texas. Primary sources and excellent bibliography.

Joutel, Henri, Johanna S. Warren (Translator). William C. Foster, (Editor). *The La Salle Expedition to Texas: The Journal of Henri Joutel, 1684–1687.* Texas State Historical Association, 1998. Adult. Primary source; journal by member of the La Salle expedition.

Gilmore, Kathleen. K. "Treachery and Tragedy in the Texas Wilderness." *Bulletin of the Texas Archeological Society* 69 (1998): 35–46. Adult. Account of the murder of La Salle in East Texas.

La Salle in Texas: A Multicultural Historical Reenactment. San Antonio, Institute of Texan Cultures, 2000. Intermediate/youth. A mock trial of the members of the La Salle expedition (including the Talon children) who returned to France. Well-organized with detailed roles and background provided.

Mitchell, Mark G. *Raising* La Belle. Austin, Texas: Eakin Press, 2002. Intermediate/youth. An account of the excavation of *La Belle* intertwined with the story of La Salle. Written for a middle school audience.

Muhlstein, Anke. *La Salle: Explorer of North American Frontier.* New York: Arcade, 1994. Adult. Detailed story of the life of La Salle.

Parkman, Francis. *La Salle and the Discovery of the Great West.* 1889. Reprint. New York: New American Library, 1963. Adult. Classic history of La Salle.

Payment, Simone. *La Salle: Claiming the Mississippi River for France.* New York: The Rosen Publishing Group, Inc. 2004. Intermediate/youth. Well-written story of La Salle with colorful illustrations.

Weddle, Robert S. *The French Thorn: Rival Explorers in the Spanish Sea, 1682–1762.* College Station: Texas A&M University Press, 1991. Adult. Excellent history of La Salle in Spanish territory and their response.

Zronik, John. *Sieur de La Salle: New World Adventurer.* New York: Crabtree Publishing Company, 2006. Intermediate/youth. Colorful, well-illustrated story of La Salle. Written for intermediate students.

Unit Four — *SURVIVING ALONG THE GULF COAST*

Ancona, George. *Powwow.* New York: Harcourt Brace and Company, 1993. Intermediate/youth. Rich in photographs of modern-day powwows.

Bolton, Herbert E. *The Hasinais: S. Caddoan as Seen by the First Europeans.* Norman: University of Oklahoma Press, 1987. Adult. Well-documented history of the contact period in Texas.

Carter, Cecile Elkins. *Caddo Indians: Where We Came From.* Norman: University of Oklahoma Press, 1995. Adult. A history of the tribe written by a Caddo historian.

Chipman, Donald and Harriet Joseph. *Explorers and Settlers of Spanish Texas.* Austin: UT Press, 2001. Intermediate/youth. Written for middle school students. Focus on the individuals who came to Texas.

Foster, William C. ed. *Save the Young: The 1691 Expedition of Captain Martinez to Rescue the Last Survivors at Fort St. Louis, Texas.* Corpus Christi: American Binding and Publishing, 2004. Adult. The diary of Martinez with a preface and introduction by Foster. Text in English and Spanish.

Foster, William C., ed. *The La Salle Expedition in Texas: The Journal of Henri Joutel, 1684–1687.* Austin: TSHA, 1998. Adult. Primary source for information about the French. Written by La Salle's second-in-command.

Hickerson, Nancy Parrott. *The Jumanos: Hunters and Traders of the South Plains.* Austin: UT Press, 1994. Adult. Story of the Native American group known as Jumano.

Kenmotsu, Nancy. "Seeking Friends, Avoiding Enemies." Austin: *Bulletin of the Texas Archeological Society,* Vol. 72 pp. 24–35, 2001. Adult. Well-documented article using Spanish documents to trace the settlements and travel of the Jumano tribe.

La Vere, David. *The Texas Indians.* College Station: Texas A&M University Press, 2004.

Newcomb, W.W. Jr. *The Indians of Texas.* Austin: UT Press, 1961. Adult. Classic history of Native Americans; prehistoric, contact, and historic.

Perttula, Timothy K. *The Caddo Nation.* Austin: UT Press, 1992. Adult. Well-researched, includes historic and archeological sources.

O'Connor, Kathryn S. *The Presidio La Bahia del Espiritu Santo, 1721 to 1846.* Austin: Von Boeckmann-Jones, 1966. Adult. The story of the Presidio and its various locations.

Ricklis, Robert. *The Karankawa Indians.* Austin: UT Press, 1996. Adult. Excellent reference based on archeological sources.

Smith, F. Todd. *The Caddo Indians: Tribes at the Convergence of Empires 1542–1854.* College Station: Texas A&M University Press, 1995. Adult. Well researched with detailed maps, notes, and bibliography.

Turner, E. Sue and Thomas R. Hester. *A Field Guide to Stone Artifacts.* Austin: Texas Monthly, 1985. Adult. Descriptions and sketches of early stone tools in Texas.

Weddle, Robert S. ed. *La Salle, the Mississippi, and the Gulf: Three Primary Documents.* College Station: Texas A&M University Press, 1987. Adult. Primary sources for the story of the Talon children who sailed with La Salle and returned to France.

Yolen, Jane. *Encounter.* New York: Harcourt Brace, 1992. Intermediate to elementary. Describes the meeting of Columbus and Native Americans from the viewpoint of a Taino boy. Available in Spanish and French.

EPILOGUE

Bruseth, James E. and Toni S. Turner. *From A Watery Grave: The Discovery and Excavation of La Salle's Shipwreck,* La Belle. College Station: Texas A & M University Press, 2005.

Foster, William C., ed. *The La Salle Expedition to Texas: The Journal of Henri Joutel, 1684–87.* Austin: Texas State Historical Association, 1998.

Foster, William C., ed. *Save the Young: The 1691 Expedition of Captain Martinez to Rescue the Last Survivors of the Massacre at Fort St. Louis, Texas.* Corpus Christi: American Binding and Printing, 2004. Available from the Museum of the Coastal Bend, Victoria.

Gilmore, Kathleen K. "Treachery and Tragedy in the Texas Wilderness." *Bulletin of the Texas Archeological Society,* Volume 69, pp. 35–46 (with King H. Gill). Austin: Texas Archeological Society, 1998.

Gilmore, Kathleen. "People of La Salle's Last Expedition," *Bulletin of the Texas Archeological Society,* Volume 76, pp. 107–121. Austin: Texas Archeological Society, 2005.

Weddle, R. S. ed. "La Salle's Survivors." *Southwest Historical Quarterly* Vol. 75(4). Austin: Texas State Historical Association, 1972.

Weddle, R. S. *La Salle, the Mississippi and the Gulf: Three Primary Documents.* College Station: Texas A&M University Press, 1987.